D0676718

3 7910 99005816 3

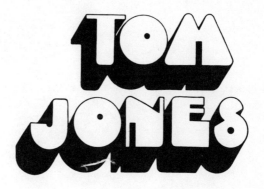

PETER JONES

Henry Regnery Company • Chicago

CONTENTS

1 Superstar

Once upon a not-so-long-ago, the word *star* was strong enough and explicit enough to describe a top-class performer in almost any field—films, sports, pop music. One had to work hard, usually for years, to become a star, not just an actor, a player, or a singer.

The word implied a special kind of magic, something original and instantly recognizable that lifted the star from the rest of the herd. In its dictionary sense a star is a shining celestial body, a twinkling point of light; in its show business sense: a celebrated, outstanding figure.

But pop music, with its never-ending sagas of the overnight successes and the "don't care about tomorrow," never was built on modesty; so the word *star* was used incautiously to say the least. The ballyhoo boys of publicity and the fast hype, looking for the overnight success to build an overnight fortune, used *star* to describe almost any newcomer, no matter how limited the talent or how brief the necessary experience. The word simply failed to do its job, which was to separate the extra special from the routine.

Any lucky lad, hauled into the recording studios straight from hollering hopefully in his local coffee bar or "discovered" singing while he worked behind the counter of a supermarket, was hailed as a star, almost before he'd discovered which was the business end of a microphone. That's how pop music developed. Each new "find" was found more spectacularly than the one who went before.

Any kid with the right looks and personality could be plugged mercilessly as the new star. The description was soon meaningless. It was used, abused, and finally ignored.

Yet every so often new artists broke through, shouldered through the lines by the weight of an exceptional talent. They simply had to be separated, by a word, from the rest of the hopeful Toms, Dicks, and Harrys.

In the year 1965, it was a Tom. Tom Jones. A name so common back in his native Wales that it was surprising he had shortened his full name, Thomas James Woodward. After all, Tommy Woodward wasn't all that undistinguished a name. And it was a real name, not one of those descriptive dynamic made-up names that pop music was constantly throwing up. We'd had them all—a Power, an Eager, a Goode, a Wilde, a Fury.

But Tom Jones it was to be. It rang a bell right away, because there was a tremendously successful movie of the same name going the rounds. The film was extra special, and this new boy singer was extra special. He grabbed pop music, then in the grip of long-haired groups—grabbed it by the scruff of the neck and didn't let go.

Having shaken it up, he injected virility, toughness, roughness, and sheer, unadulterated sex. His impact was so great and so immediate that the word *star* seemed even more inadequate. If a kid who had cooed his way into the Top Twenty with a voice that wouldn't travel ten yards without a microphone and two hundred watts of amplification was being called a star, then Tom Jones had to be called something else. Tom the Tiger was soon the leader of the pack, the one out in front in terms of vocal and visual impact. Adjectives were sought, found, and rejected.

Then the industry hit on the right word to describe his impact round the world. Tom was the first British *superstar*.

The six-footer with the crinkly black hair crashed manfully into the Top Twenty in Britain in 1965 and has been there ever since. That first hit record, "It's Not Unusual," wasn't just unusual, it was downright astonishing. He'd come, apparently, from out of nowhere. It was the right song at the right time and even knowledgeable pop people, the experts, assumed that this performance, marked by a clear feel for the blues and studded with high-voltage personality, was by a black singer from the United States. For sure there wasn't anybody in Britain who could get a raw-edged sound like that.

As the song hit the charts, show business writers dug

desperately for information on the man who sang with such muscularity. They called him Tiger Tom, and they were amazed when they unearthed details of his background: a white boy who had been a construction laborer in Wales. They discovered that he was born in 1940, which meant that if he had been singing during his twenty-five years, something had gone wrong with the talent-spotting system.

Anyway, the experts were glad to see him. Maybe this was the first move forward of an attempt to end the domination of the groups, with their eternal, infernal guitar and drums and the sounds that never seemed to change.

Ever since the Beatles, in 1962, had first tentatively staked a claim in the charts with "Love Me Do," then stormed to the top with "Please Please Me," and then done pretty well what they liked with the pop industry, the talent-spotting moguls had been at each other's throats to find equally distinguished groups. The Beatles' young manager, Brian Epstein, went on to produce Gerry and the Pacemakers and Billy J. Kramer and the Dakotas (plus one of the few girl singers to be even tolerated at big-selling level, the likable Cilla Black). Liverpool was well and truly on the map, and the world knew of the River Mersey and the Cavern Club and the curious nasally pungent accents that came from those parts. But everywhere everybody was trying to leap on the bandwagon that the Beatles had started.

When Tom Jones and "It's Not Unusual" started climbing to the top, the groups had it all their own way. In that particular week when Tom dented the Top Ten for the first time, there were hits registered by the Seekers, Wayne Fontana and the Mindbenders, the Animals, the Kinks, Herman's Hermits, the Rolling Stones, the Hollies, Manfred Mann, the Shadows, the Who, the Ivy League—all British and generally rated as the best in the world. Why, there was even an all-girl vocal-instrumental team, Goldie and the Gingerbreads. They happened to come from the United States, but they were based in Britain, where it was all happening in pop music.

The business needed a solo singer with an unusual touch to break the boring pattern. In the era of Elvis Presley and "Heartbreak Hotel," the American side of pop was on top; the Beatles reversed the balance of power. Tom Jones was to upset things a little bit more.

In early 1965, when Tom's record thudded onto critics' desks along with about fifty other discs released that week, few would have given a "new" solo male singer much chance of making it to the top. In Britain there was Cliff Richard, and everywhere there was Elvis, and the rest were nowhere in terms of consistency.

Consequently, maybe it is understandable that most record reviewers underestimated the potential impact of the newcomer with the rampaging style on what seemed at best an above-average song. "It's Not Unusual," he belted, and okay it was miles away from the normal sugary approach of a British balladeer, but was it likely to get itself even heard among the glut of groups?

Still, that voice seemed to owe something to hard-core rock and roll, something to the blues, something to the

United States, and a helluva lot to a hard-driving backing, polished and repolished to propel the singer along at maximum power.

Yet the song didn't instantly fit into any current category, and most critics missed it as a potential hit. That's one of the hazards of trying to review all the releases on a week's list. So many records, so many advance publicity puffs "guaranteeing" that so-and-so will be the greatest that sometimes, quite unintentionally, the critical faculties are blunted, numbed, destroyed.

But the British public took to "It's Not Unusual" right away. It hit the lower end of the Top Thirty, leapfrogged to number ten and then number two. Then it was top of the pile. The disc jockeys, most of them slow off the mark in this case, took to it and whipped up more interest. The Jones boy known as Tiger Tom was rushed round the newspaper offices to meet the influential journalists who would add the written word to the rest of the action. Pictures, proving that he was a tough-looking but handsome lad and definitely not black, were printed. The buildup was on, as it had been a few thousand times since the Beatles had revolutionized the record industry.

Right from the start it was obvious that Tom would not allow himself to be a one-hit wonder. There had been dozens of that kind of singer, too, in pop music, kids who struck it rich by coming out with the right sound at the right time, only then to find that their basic talents were not strong enough to enable them to sustain their disc-selling status.

6

Tom looked, talked, sang like the real professional. He sang because he loved singing, he said. Sure the money he could expect from royalties and personal appearances was useful, but what was wrong with singing even for nothing if you were a Welshman, through and through? In Wales, when coal-miners weren't mining, they were singing—natural tenors and natural sentimentalists, all of them. To hear a Welsh crowd sing out at a Rugby football International, for instance, is one of the most stirring sounds in the world of sports. They sing and their voices ring out round the valleys, and just for a few moments, the sweat and strain of grubbing coal are forgotten.

But they'd not really produced a world-class pop singer. Welsh heroes were rugby players, soccer players, and the occasional classical or operatic singer; the rest were amateur vocalists. Now they had someone else to sing and shout about. They had a superstar and he was Welsh and he talked about Wales and he was one of them, even though he was up there toppling the pop stars from London and Liverpool.

In fact, it came as a real surprise to know that Tom had been singing his heart out for years, just waiting for someone to acknowledge the sheer excitement of his style. He could pack more fervor into just one chorus than many of the namby-pamby mob (though classified as stars) could in an hour-long show on stage. Tom had been kept going by plain, blind, dogged, dogmatic faith in his own ability. There was one time when he thought about suicide, so great was his frustration—but that is an incident to come later in this story of a superstar.

Tom Jones knew he had something extra to offer as a singer, and he was driven on by the basic need to get that extra something recognized. Otherwise, he figured, he'd end up with a life full of sheer hard physical labor, digging ditches or humping bricks. Nobody can say for sure what it is that creates this self-confidence, especially when it seems the world just doesn't care. Tom had it, a large helping of it, and it sustained him.

He had studied the pop music business, albeit from afar. He had a large collection of records by the great American rhythm and blues stars. He wore them wafer thin as he listened for clues as to what made the singers tick, what helped them communicate so that their music lifted his own pulse rate and stirred his own heartbeats. What made a black man sing differently from a white man? Was it a matter of heritage, tradition, background? Or was it that he let his soul take over? Whatever it was, Tom wanted a share of it. He listened and tapped his feet and snapped his fingers, and if he never found the answer in just a word or phrase, he soaked up the atmosphere that came out of his record player.

In 1965 Tom was getting a share of the adulation he heaped on his own favorite singers. People wanted to know about this man called Jones. The more cynical expected him to dream up a suitably glamorous background, maybe a story of a sensational slice of luck that led to his discovery, but Tom didn't bother with the slick story that could bring the biggest headlines. With the advice of his manager, another Welshman who sang, Gordon Mills, plus some of the best brains in the business, Tom managed to remain himself.

Sure Tom talked openly about his background. He talked, too, of what he wanted to achieve, and if his personal targets seemed out of the Impossible Dream category, there was always humility. And no matter how big he talked about his hopes, he could never have known, then, just how much impact he would have on world-class show business.

What's more, he would have thought his friends were crazy if they'd predicted that he would, in a few short years, be starring in the plushest of the Las Vegas cabarets, be shaking hands on equal terms with his long-time idol, Elvis Presley, and be hearing Frank Sinatra describe him as "number one."

One can dream, all right. Dreams can be a solace, a consolation. But even dreams have some kind of limit, beyond which the imagination just can't stretch. Mostly Tom's imagination didn't reach much further than a determination to stay in the business that had brought him fame. He basked in the happiness of having total strangers come up to him in the street and congratulate him on his hit record.

To be realistic, even the most patriotic of British show business bigots could not have guessed Tom's international potential. The really big music stars generally came from the United States. The visit of a topliner from the other side of the Atlantic was still an occasion, a thrill. Very few big names in Britain had the sort of style or personality to enable them to travel the world and see their names in six-foot-high neon lights outside the mink and champagne haunts of the world's wealthy.

In pop itself there were the Beatles and the Rolling Stones, yes—but there were four and five of them and so potential audience appeal was split up and added to. Each of the Beatles—John Lennon, Paul McCartney, George Harrison, Ringo Starr—had a personal following. But solo performers capable of packing any kind of auditorium were so hard to find in Britain that they could be counted on the fingers of one hand.

This, then, was the show business scene on which Tom Jones appeared. In music, there was no sign that the groups were losing fans, though many were getting tired of the three-chord trickery of the guitarists, the insipid performances, and the incredible clothes, trappings, and trimmings of something that was quickly going stale yet was latching onto any gimmick to survive for a few more months.

It was reasonable to think that the groups were thought to be good because there was safety in numbers. Spread the action around and poor stage presentations weren't so bad, and if the sound wasn't good enough, well . . . make it loud and no one will notice with all that screaming and weeping and stage-invading. With the noisy accessories of a pop-group show, fans couldn't see that most of their heroes just didn't sound as good in person as they did on records.

The groups were split between the good and the bad, and there weren't enough good ones. What was needed was a new solo personality—a new Sinatra, or Presley, or even an emotional storm like Johnnie Ray, the original "Cry Guy" who packed theaters on a shower of real tears but had long since vanished to leave a void in the area of way-out pop showmanship.

Superstar

But along came Tom Jones, Superstar. He brought toughness and vitality and masculinity and simple physical power to a sensation-happy area of the entertainment industry. Anybody who thinks it all happened easily just doesn't know what pop singing is really all about.

This is the story of Tom Jones, the highest-paid entertainer ever in British show business, and of the pop music scene he came to dominate. If sometimes truth does seem stranger than fiction, well . . . that's only to be expected when you shadow a superstar as he stalks aggressively round the world.

2 Up from the Pit

Tom Jones was born June 7, 1940, in Treforrest, Glamorgan, some nine months after the start of World War II. His parents, Tom and Freda Woodward, were pleased to have a son in addition to their daughter, but feeding an extra mouth was inevitably a burden. Not only was money in short supply, but so was food in the days of rationing and tighten-your-belt-to-help-the-war-effort.

What's more, there never was much real peace of mind for a mining family because there was always the very real risk of an accident down the pit. Tom's dad was lucky. He worked hard, but he kept out of harm's way. Many of his friends were injured, some killed, as they hacked away at the backbreaking job of fulfilling their quota of coal-digging hundreds of feet below the earth's surface.

Tom was a beautiful child. As a toddler, his smile

was cheeky, face fringed by curls of hair much lighter and looser than they are today. When he was eight, his curls were looser still, parted high over the left ear, and there were signs of that juttingly aggressive jaw, plus the makings of the smile that was to captivate several million women the world over. It always was an expressive face, lit most of the time by a smile that was reflected instantly in the eyes. A self-mocking face, often the sort of face that states clearly that there is mischief ahead, and only Tom in the whole world knew where and when it was going to start.

Often Tom would go to see his father off to the pits, even when he had to get up by five o'clock to be ready to shoot down the mine-shaft by seven o'clock. Sometimes Tom would act out a charade, wearing his dad's mining boots, just as any child likes to share somehow in what his father does for a living.

Tom sang; every Welsh child does. He sang then in a high-pitched voice that had an almost angelic quality to it. It wasn't long before he started showing that extrovert flash of personality that all true stars eventually need. At school he needed no hard-sell persuasion to sing in the choir, and it was safest to let him sing solo if he felt like it, because Tom could raise his own form of hell even as a kid.

His headmaster at primary school, hearing Tom sing "The Lord's Prayer" one day, was amazed at the intuitive way the boy made it sound like something out of a revivalist Gospel meeting.

Tom's sister, Sheila, tried to maintain the right balance of power for a girl six years older than her brother, but there were the inevitable quarrels because nobody could keep Tom subdued for long. But he had a zany sense of humor, and he never bore a grudge; soon the two of them would be laughing together, all differences patched up.

All in all, it was a happy, song-filled childhood, albeit in a far from wealthy household. His mother has said: "Obviously parents are always likely to be wise after the event, but I know most of the people back home had an idea that Tom was something special as a singer.

"When we went on a family outing, say to a wedding, he'd be dead keen to get up and sing. He knew most of the popular songs of the day off by heart and it always made us feel good to see the confident way he'd get up to sing them."

And the folk down Pontypridd way still remember how Tom would go to the local grocer's shop, prop himself up on a wooden box, and just sing away. Certainly those who live along Laura Road, Treforrest, are proudest of all, because they watched Tom grow up from short-trousered schoolboy, to working lad, to married man, and then, in what seemed to them like the blinking of an eye, to superstar

As Tom sang, more for practice than for reward, his father went on digging out some fourteen tons of coal a day. When Tom was in his early teens, his dad exhorted his boy not to follow him down the pits. He'd tell Tom, "Keep at your singing, boy. For a lad like you, there's no future down the pits. Once you're down there, it gets into the system and it's like there's no escape. You just keep going as you are. I want you to do something

15

better and if that thing is singing . . . well, I'm behind you all the way."

So Tom sang. With parental approval it was easy finding somewhere to sing. Many top singers sang against their parents' wishes, and the restrictions made the struggle for recognition harder. Tom remembers with gratitude the way his parents believed in him and his voice.

But Tom had to earn a wage in addition to the few cents he picked up singing. For a while he was in a leather goods factory as an apprentice glove cutter, earning less than $5 a week despite his enthusiasm for the job. His wages increased substantially, to about $36 a week, when he worked on a building site, but as he has said many times since, "Singing songs is a lot less exhausting than carrying bricks around." The inevitable reward for hod carrying was an aching body; the penalty for too much singing was maybe a sore throat.

The very toughness of his background meant that Tom was always able to look after himself. There were gang fights, but they always stopped on the right side of the law. Tom recalled this side of his youth in an interview with Jack Bentley, of the London *Sunday Mirror*, and agreed that he was one of the lucky ones. So many other kids from similar backgrounds moved from street corner brawls into full-time crime.

Yet if he was useful enough with his fists when the occasion called for it (and that was regrettably often), he was even more useful with his voice. For a time he sang in the bar of a public house, the Wheatsheaf, blasting out Top Twenty tunes just to raise the price of a pint of beer.

Up from the Pit

Brian Pitman, a long-time friend of Tom, told *Disc* magazine that Tom had been ill for two years during his schooldays, suffering from tuberculosis.

"He didn't really have much time for school," Pitman said, "except that he was always very good at drawing. And singing. But when he started singing properly, he used to pack 'em in at the Wheatsheaf. Originally he started doing these shows just to get some beer money."

Brian worked with Tom on the building sites and also helped him find jobs outside. But Tom was hard to please. Most of the other jobs lasted just a couple of weeks or so. Then he'd quit for no apparent reason except simple boredom, and he'd live on his unemployment compensation plus the few cents he earned from his singing.

During the years of indecision about employment, Tom learned to play drums, and that again helped to develop his sense of rhythm—develop a sense of rhythm because you can't really be taught, it comes instinctively from within, you can only develop it. It was there in Tom, deep down inside, and he needed only practice and self-confidence to bring it out.

That public house atmosphere certainly helped Tom develop his style. Particularly on paydays the place was crowded with coal-dust-covered men from the pits, all lads together, playing darts and cards and wallowing in the conviviality induced by a succession of quickly downed pints of ale after a hard day in the pit.

They liked Tom because he was really one of them, even if he never did go down the mines; they applauded the ferocious way he attacked the songs of the day. Tom, however, *had* to work at full volume in order to

17

make himself heard above the din. Another way of attracting attention was to swivel the hips a bit in the way established by Elvis. He pointed the lyrics with sharp, stabbing hand gestures. Even as a semi-professional entertainer, Tom had learned that it was a good thing to put on a show that was visually worth watching and still keep his voice working full force.

That was in 1957, and there were Elvis Presley and Bill Haley and the Comets. The big beat was the thing. It was the time of "Rock Around the Clock" and "Shake, Rattle and Roll"; the skiffle era, the day of the hillbilly song in Britain, had been and was, largely, gone. Tom knew a lot about Lonnie Donegan and hits such as "Rock Island Line": skiffle had triggered a whole do-it-yourself era in popular music. Thousands of youngsters backed their cultivated nasal hillbilly style of singing with homemade tea chest basses and cheap guitars.

Meanwhile, black American artists, such as Fats Domino and Little Richard, continued weaving their spells on Tom. Even greater was the influence of Sam Cooke, who was building up millions of sales for titles such as "You Send Me" and "I'll Come Running Back to You."

Pop was going through a really exciting period. It wasn't only good to listen to, it was emotional and it was exciting to dance to. And Tom spent a lot of his time in the local dance halls, rock-and-rolling like a dervish, commanding more than his fair share of floor space when his legs really got going. It was all part of the pattern. He was developing his sense of rhythm, force feeding the style that was to make him one of the most exciting onstage performers in show business history.

18

When Tom really got into a rocking mood, he virtually needed a whole ballroom to himself.

He was growing up fast, physically, socially, and mentally. He learned to sink a fast pint of ale and to come out with an instant crack. His was the language of the mining districts, and he was most definitely nowhere in the running for the "Best Dressed Man in Wales" title. Rockers (and he was definitely a rocker) went for the way-out gear.

Later, a journalist was to write: "At last, in Tom Jones, a man has risen in a profession which for too long has been dominated by boys." It was in those years, around Pontypridd, South Wales, that Tom developed his masculinity and his manhood. There was no room for the weakling because life was built on a constant battle. And in any battle there's little sympathy for the loser.

All that depressed Tom, as he wandered back to his tiny terraced cottage home after a night of singing and supping was that he felt convinced that he'd never get the sort of acclaim for his singing that his family and friends felt he deserved.

He has said, "There were many times when I would just have chucked it all in. You find that you can do well, handle an audience and you feel that one day it'll all come right. But you hear someone else's record coming across on the radio and you realise that you're just a semi-professional in a professional world. What kept me going was local encouragement, specially from my dad. You keep thinking about a lucky break and wondering if it will ever come. It was worse, really, being away there in Wales, when all the pop music thing was so definitely in London. But it would have taken tremendous confidence on my part to have made the break and gone to London on my own. I had commitments and I felt at least secure in Wales . . ."

Tom's first paid appearance, at a local working men's club, brought him a crisp £1 note for the performance of six songs. He felt, just for a moment, that this payment made him a professional. A £1 note didn't go far when spent on a round of drinks, but Tom felt proud. It wasn't the size of the fee, just the fact that he was being paid for doing something he'd loved doing all his life.

At that time he was working as Tommy Scott, for no particular reason except that the name appealed to him. When Tom finished the nightly stints at the Wheatsheaf, he organized a group because he knew that groups were becoming the big thing in pop music.

His group, such as it was, went through several name changes, too. They were the Playboys and the Senators and eventually the Squires.

An interesting theory about how Tom built his stage movements came from Chris Slade, drummer with the Squires, who was interviewed in *Disc* magazine in 1968 and said: "Originally those gestures and movements came because he guided us into numbers. One hand raised meant go it faster, another movement meant make it slower, and he'd put his foot down on stage to mean something else.

"Tom was billed as the Twisting Vocalist and it didn't matter much that we didn't play so well. This was rock and roll. Tom always projected himself well—he picked up all the new American dances and used them on stage."

So the fight for recognition went on and on. Tom and the group enjoyed good audiences and good reactions from them, but Tom Jones, alias Tommy Scott, knew that a recording contract and fame were still miles away. It was galling to him because there was so much rubbish being recorded. True, the artists had both the advantage of top recording studio facilities and professional advice, but they still couldn't start to match the excitement generated by Tom and his group in 1963.

It seemed that there were at least a million groups and that at least half of them were making records. Tom had met with several people who pushed forward and offered to manage his affairs, but Wales was too far from London, where everything was happening. Oddly enough, one group making it big with a record at the time were Los Indios Tabajaras, with a melody called "Maria Elena," and the story was that they were Mexican Indians who lived in the jungle and happened to find a couple of guitars and learned to play and created their own brand of music. The jungles of Central America . . . and yet they had a recording contract. Tom, only a short way from London, comparatively speaking, must have felt he was a million miles away for all the interest the recording bosses were taking in him.

Tom was a Teddy boy, in the fashion of the early sixties, no doubt about that: he wore the long drape jackets with the velvet collars and the drainpipe trousers and the platform shoes and his hair was long and well greased. He's said that he started drinking at the age

21

of fourteen, simply because he looked older. He may have kept out of trouble, but he certainly looked fearsome—broken nose and all—and he looked as if he could cause a whole lot of bother if anybody riled him.

In a *Sunday Mirror* interview, Tom admitted: "Once I got near to killing a couple of fellers. Look at this nose. It's been broken so many times in scraps that I can't even remember the particular punch-up which made it this shape. The boot and butting were all part of the fight. I pulled every dirty trick in the book. You had to if you wanted to come out alive."

But he stressed also that he didn't go out of his way to find trouble. He thought sometimes that he had the sort of face that asked for trouble, even without trying. "The police were always on the lookout for me, but I got away with most things, like getting into a cinema without paying."

Once Tom saw a close girl friend walking along the street with another boy. He said: "I went mad. I almost beat him into a pulp. Some weeks later I got into another punch-up. Some feller, who wanted to have a go because I done up one of his mates, butted me through a fish and chip shop window. When I scrambled out in a blind rage, covered in glass and ready to do him, I saw two cops standing there. They said if I laid a finger on him they'd run me in."

Later, Tom gave a revealing insight into how he saw life in the Welsh valleys. He said that "I didn't half fancy myself, you know. But you know I always wanted to be a real man, wanted to prove myself. Being a boy in the valleys is like being a young buck in a Red Indian

22

tribe. It's a man's world and you have to fight to wear your feathers. That's what gets my goat about the long hair bit being some kind of protest or sign of talent."

Tom rarely spoke out again about his tearaway days as he did in that interview. It wasn't a matter of trying to avoid the truth, just that he passed into a world where it paid to have a sense of responsibility and where, anyway, the very reasons for getting into a fight had been removed. But his statement pinpointed the driving force that was to take Tom to the top. He was prepared to fight and claw every inch of the way to reach his target: stardom. It didn't take any effort at all on his part to forget all about going down the mines, and he pushed aside, effortlessly, the memory of his distant past of muscle-searing days on the building sites.

His aim was quite clear. Armed with an abundance of personal confidence, he was going to make a go of the pop music business, no matter how long it took him. All he needed was the break, the helping hand from somebody smart enough to promote this rough and raw talent from Wales.

As it happens, he didn't have to wait too much longer.

3 Enter a Manager

One night in 1964 Tom Jones was singing at the Pontypridd Working Men's Club. It was pretty much like any other night in town—a small pay packet at the end of it, a responsive audience but with the drinks flowing and the artists having to pull out every stop to register.

A pretty average scene, in fact. But one man took a close interest in Tom's performance. Actually, this man had come to see one of the people involved in the Profumo scandal, Mandy Rice-Davies, in cabaret, but she was unable to be there and he'd idly stayed on to see what else was happening. Tom Jones, then still Tommy Scott, was what was happening!

Gordon Mills was Welsh and good-looking, and he had an eye for talent. He was the sort of man who stood out in a crowd. Shy on the surface, he had something about him that inspired confidence.

Gordon Mills knew a lot about show business. He'd won a national championship as a harmonica player and he'd joined a vaudeville group known as Morton Fraser's Harmonica Gang. The act was a mixture of music and comedy, and it had toured the music halls for years and years, changing personnel regularly because it was a routine sort of act basically. The routine was stifling to anybody with a spark of ambition. Gordon stood it as long as he could, then split with a couple of friends to form their own vocal-instrumental trio, the Viscounts.

Three good-looking guys, with a flair for comedy and some expertise on harmonicas—the ingredients were right and they won a recording contract, with a couple of records getting onto the charts. Certainly, the group came over well on television. There was a professionalism about their routines, combining musicianship with agility, and their voices harmonized well.

Their success didn't last long, however, because the restless Gordon Mills wanted to move on yet again; he had a feeling that he could go it alone. His songwriting was developing well, and he also had his eye on some talent he felt could be promoted. Gordon didn't have a great deal of money to set up his own business, but he certainly did have belief in his own ability to succeed.

So this was the man who sat in that Pontypridd club, unknown to the rest of the audience. And this was the man who was instantly convinced that Tom Jones was a superstar in embryo. What impressed him was the way Tom moved around onstage, helping out his vocal attack on the lyrics with his persistent body swinging.

He believed that Tom had a tremendous sense of rhythm and exceptional accuracy of pitch as he soared and walloped into a succession of familiar, mostly up-tempo songs.

Gordon contacted Tom after the show, along with the Jones group, and tried to persuade all five of them to go to London right away and take a chance on making themselves a quick fortune. Gordon really did believe that stardom was not far away, especially for Tom, but unfortunately that was a story Tom had heard all too often before.

He said: "You get in a drinking club and there's always somebody who gets carried away by the drink or something and he comes up and offers to be your manager. Then, next morning, in the sobering up bit, they don't think it's such a good idea, so you hear nothing more. Nothing lost, for them. It's your hopes they've raised."

Yet there was something different about this man Mills. He didn't harp on the financial rewards that Tom and the boys could almost certainly be "guaranteed." He played it more from the heart—that they deserved to be recognized in the pop world and that he thought he could help. He sounded sincere, and it didn't sound like a put-up job. So in the end, the Tom Jones entourage decided it was worth stringing along with this fellow Welshman.

The name Tommy Scott was changed to Tom Jones, and some weeks later Tom and the Squires trekked up to London, hoping that at last a miracle would happen and they would find stardom. The first few months in

London proved that Tom's personal toughness was going to be tested to the full. Life became one long round of auditions and recording tests and days of waiting while the so-called shrewd folk of the industry dreamed up reasons for not accepting the group.

The fact that the group business was thinning out was against them. There had been a couple of years when just about anything could get into the charts, but now, spearheaded by the Beatles, there was a demand for greater quality.

Among them there was about $120 a week available, and that was paid from Gordon Mills's own bank account. After all, he figured, he'd persuaded the boys to give up some security in Wales and it was only right that he lay out the cash to ensure that they would have something to eat every day. As Tom has said since, "We weren't exactly making it in Wales, but at least we had day-time jobs, and what's more, some of the people locally were beginning to look on us as good entertainers."

The boys lived in a small furnished flat at Shepherd's Bush. They collected all the weekly bills together and shared all the expenses. Tom urgently needed some more money one day and approached the normally sympathetic Gordon. Though he eventually got the money, he was left in no doubt that Gordon himself was running up a substantial overdraft, yet there was still no sign of the breakthrough that could give the boys a chance to make a record.

What made it worse was the constant questioning from back home in Wales. "How's it going, Tom?"

asked the family. "Any news yet? When are we going to hear your records on the radio?" Running off and looking for fame and fortune is fine, but you always leave behind some people who are ready to rub it in if you don't actually find it. There is nothing worse than the galling experience of reporting failure to one's folks and friends, and enemies positively revel in the news.

During this period Tom Jones actually thought of committing suicide. Later, in an interview with Alan Walsh for *Melody Maker*, Tom said, "Yes, I definitely thought about suicide as I stood there on the platform of Notting Hill Underground station in London. The thought was there all right. I don't know to this day whether I would have done it, but the thought was there in my head. I just wondered what was the point of my going on. I just felt at the lowest point of despair."

This story is confirmed in the Tom Jones color magazine published in 1969. Certainly it underlines the sheer feeling of strain that this normally resilient Welshman experienced as he saw both time and money slipping away from him, tumbling him further away from his aim of somehow making the big time in show business.

Strangely enough, one thing that worked against Tom was the very fact that he was so resolutely masculine and tough—a no-nonsense character who had clearly learned a lot in the University of Life, if not in the usual academies of learning.

For pop music seemed to be more and more dominated by the very young. Tom, at twenty-four, was almost an old man to be starting a recording career. There had been twelve-year-old kids in the charts, names like Jackie Dennis, a kilted lad from Scotland, and Laurie London spring to mind. Laurie had a world-wide hit with "He's Got the Whole World in His Hands," then faded. He returned, momentarily, and showed that he'd developed a well-rounded, mature voice, but there were no more hits—it's as if one really does get only one bite at the cherry in pop music. One flop for a one-time chart-topper can be the end of the road.

Suddenly there was a worthwhile gimmick in being a sub-teenager in a kilt, dancing about a stage, or in being almost any young kid suddenly boosted to temporary fame on the strength of a catchy little song. But Tom didn't have any such gimmicks going for him. True, he moved like an athlete of song onstage and he had a good voice. But where, agents wanted to know, were the real gimmicks? Perhaps if Tiger Tom had walked on for auditions towing a couple of real tigers behind him, his voice would have been noticed. Instead, he felt in a strange middle world—a bit too old to join in and a bit too young to give up.

He even got involved in the disastrously frustrating world of demonstration discs. This was a heartbreaking business, especially for an ambitious singer, because he was really only singing so that a writer or publisher could have a vehicle for one of his songs.

Eventually, the records were played over to big-time stars, who would then make the decision whether or not to record the material. In a sense, he was helping others to make a name, but he was doing so in a completely anonymous way.

It was a matter of "This is my new song—so how do

you like it?" rather than "This is my new song, performed by Tom Jones, and how do you like him?" But there is a saying that everything comes to him who waits. Tom had done the waiting and now was just waiting for the "coming." Through sheer persistence on the part of Gordon Mills, he landed a recording contract with Decca in London, and his first record was "Chills and Fever."

It would be nice to say "Chills and Fever" made a tremendous impact on the public. It would be nice, but it wouldn't be remotely truthful. Anyway, making impact wouldn't have been in keeping with Tom's life and struggles at this time. Maybe it was completely predictable that it should flop. It sank virtually without trace.

Looking backward, it is hard to see just why it should have had so little impact. The same furious style of song selling was there, and it wasn't a bad number. A fair amount of care had gone into the production, but it just didn't take off. There was the odd pebble-stirring in the publicity pool to mention Tom and his record, but it needed a great deal more radio plugging and much more money for advertising for the song to make progress. After all, there were dozens of new artists making disc debuts every week, and some were being launched on such sensational gimmickry that they simply had to merit some space in the papers.

Later, Gordon Mills said: "If I'd left Tom alone, he'd probably have gone on singing the blues for the rest of time. But facts are facts. There are very few blues singers of any importance in the world today who can match the popularity of a top pop singer.

"I know that Tom was disappointed when we started

31

on records away from the blues field, but I eventually realised that it was primarily a matter of getting through to an audience."

One can imagine how the disappointment was building up in Tom's mind. Wouldn't anything go right? Hell, he'd got a disc contract after all that time and it seemed that there was a conspiracy of silence about it. "I'll show 'em," he'd said through gritted teeth as he listened to some of the watery mixtures that masqueraded as pop excitement in those days of 1964–65. To get a contract and then miss out on the opportunity was almost too much to bear. Depressed people think depressing thoughts. Many times he felt like going back to Wales—to the dole and unemployment pay, possibly, but certainly to the chance of singing his songs to his friends in the local clubs. If one has to be miserable, then it's better to be miserable with friends.

One person who had a lot of confidence that the big breakthrough was only a few minutes of disc time away was producer Peter Sullivan. Of Tom, Sullivan said: "Even at his audition for Decca, Tom showed a tremendous amount of talent. I'd been to Wales to see him work, in his own environment as it were, and the talent just glowed through, despite that wild rocker image he projected and the long hair. Somehow, he emerged as a singer who could get over the sometimes short-term effect that hit records can have on an artist's career."

In fact, although the public didn't take instantly to the Tom Jones dynamics on disc, there were people around who were able to take a long-term view of a potential big talent. For Tom, however, the failure of

"Chills and Fever" meant a return to the drawing board
—back, grudgingly, to the demonstration records he
hated, but which at least brought in a few pounds. And
it's here that his story takes a most peculiar twist.

One of his demonstration records was for a British
girl singer who was doing pretty well in the charts. It
was a song that Tom really felt he could get his teeth
into, and, coincidentally, it was written by Gordon Mills
and by Les Reed, an all-round musician who had an
acutely developed commercial turn of mind when it
came to building hit songs.

That song was "It's Not Unusual," and, for a change,
Tom really enjoyed making the demonstration disc.
There was a lot of discussion before the song was
handed over to him to use as the "A" side of his second
record for Decca, but in the end he was persuasive
enough.

Once again, the record came out without being hailed
as a sure-fire hit, mainly because Tom was still a new
name, but it was picked up by the disc jockeys, and a
substantial sum of money was spent promoting it once
it started flickering around near the foot of the charts.

Gordon Mills explained how "It's Not Unusual" was
created. "I had this phrase rushing around in my head.
Just that title phrase, which was pretty unusual because I couldn't remember anyone using it before in a
song. It was a matter of adding more to the process.
It's not unusual . . . but to what? Well, to be loved by
anyone. I thought there was a deep meaning there,
because it really is unusual to be loved, really loved, by
anyone other than sexually."

Just that one complete phrase and Gordon was more

than halfway to a massive hit. He finished the first two verses and then got together with Les Reed. The tune had been picked out mainly on C chords, but Les added a Major Seventh, which gave it a really up-to-date sound, and the whole job was finished in one hour flat. That wasn't so unusual. Many a wildly, successful pop hit is the result of just a few minutes' work after the original idea has been created. Gordon said: "I tried to sing it myself on the demonstration disc but I couldn't get the feel. Tom was around and he said he wanted to have a go at it—and that was it. It was obviously his song."

The actual recording session was over in three hours, and Tom was well on the way to his first $100,000. The record was a hit soon after its release, top in Britain and Australia, moving up fast in the United States. Gordon's view was: "There are number ones and number ones. Some just make it on the strength of a song. But Tom has made himself an artist. It's a professional recording and everything about it is good."

When it finally made the grade, Tom was justifiably knocked out. This was surely the turning-point. "It's Not Unusual" was a first-rate pop song, and it virtually became Tom's private property. Sometimes a good song is "covered" by maybe half a dozen other artists, but this one fitted Tom's style perfectly, so it would have been a waste of time for other people to try to cash in. Even now "It's Not Unusual" is used as a signature tune for his stage and television acts—Tom's way of expressing his gratitude for this comparatively simple stringing together of uncomplicated lyrics and basic melody.

34

Enter a Manager

Most British hit singles are hits only in Britain. Some, however, are shipped out all over the world and go on being successful from Oklahoma to the Orient. Tom's was just such a single. As we've seen, this was no overnight-success story. But when success struck, when Tom was paired with "It's Not Unusual," the multiple effects mushroomed.

And Tom at last had some good news to send back to Wales.

4 Women and a Wife

To tell or not to tell—that was the question. Whether it was sensible to reveal all about Tom's marriage and his young son, Mark, or whether it would be less damaging simply to keep the domestic life of the new idol hidden until the last possible moment. Nobody much worries whether a top sportsman or business tycoon has a wife and a houseful of kids, but in pop music there were divided opinions on the subject of a family.

What are the ingredients that make a top pop star? The voice, the basic talent, the ability to make commercial sounds that sell the records that earn the money. But there is something else—the question of availability and attainability. Fans flock to see the star, and most of them, way down deep inside, have the feeling that she may get to meet the idol, get romantically involved—and on such ideas were dreams built. Sometimes, even in real life, the fan got to meet and marry the leader of the band.

So in general, great security barricades had been built around married pop stars. With Sinatra, marriage didn't matter much—he was a hell raiser, a guy whose escapades with dolls had filled the gossip columns for years. And Sinatra was old, by pop standards anyway, born in December, 1915. He was twenty-eight when he won his first Gold Disc, and that was back in the war days, 1943.

Elvis Presley? In the end he got married, but that was in 1967, after he'd already had eleven years at the top, a decade-plus of even remote availability and attainability following his breakthrough with "Heartbreak Hotel." He was thirty-two when he married his Priscilla, a dark-haired girl he'd first met while doing his two-year stint as the most famous soldier in the U.S. Army. She had attended high school in Wiesbaden, Germany, where her father, an American Air Force lieutenant-colonel, was serving. It was a long courtship, but Elvis was luckier than most top pop stars in that he could keep his private life just that—private.

Until Tom happened, Elvis had set the standards for most of what happened in the teenage side of pop music. There were many who felt that when he finally said, "I do," at his wedding, his fans would say, "We don't," and would get tired of their hero and find somebody else who was available or at least seemed attainable.

And then there were the Beatles. They started the whole group industry and were built up on the boy-next-door image—which meant that they, too, were available. Attainable as well, even if the odds were about twenty million to one. Unlike the Hollywood stars of the Mighty Musical Era–stars who lived like stars and rarely rubbed shoulders with "ordinary" people— the Beatles *were* ordinary people. So were most of the other top groups. For a year or so, Beatle fans were under the impression that all four were footloose and fancy-free, unmarried, available. The few who were aware of the existence of John Lennon's lovely blonde first wife, Cynthia, and their son, Julian, just kept quiet about his family life. And that was the way it was, the way it had to be. Keep the fans building up hopes on the availability of their idols. It was all part of official pop policy.

In the end, John's "secret" wife was brought into the open, but by then, as with Elvis Presley, nothing short of total catastrophe could dent the group's popularity. Later in pop history, attitudes changed. When Elvis did marry, his home and offices were filled with good-luck messages and wedding presents from fans all over the world.

When George Harrison married his model, when Ringo Starr wed his childhood sweetheart, it was okay with the fans. Or most of them, anyway. There was a new feeling about an old idol being legally tied to just one girl. Summed up the new approach was, "He's given us a lot of pleasure and now surely he's entitled to find his own personal happiness." True, the announcement that the last bachelor Beatle, Paul Mc-Cartney, was married to an American, Linda Eastman, did cause a lot of heartbreak, but it was only a reaction reflecting that the Beatles were now four down, with none to go.

The Rolling Stones, of course, had the sort of image that didn't really involve any feeling about marriage. Brian Jones had a big personal following, but he wandered haphazardly through life, from romance to romance, and there always was an aura of impending doom over him. It was somehow predictable that his life would be short and not always sweet. And so it was. He died, drowned in the swimming pool of the first real home he'd set up since finding world stardom.

But the Stones really hinged on the appeal, the sinister and vicious sexuality, of Mick Jagger. He quite simply was a "character." He roared on, his romantic entanglements highly publicized, and he *always* seemed available—and attainable.

So attitudes eventually changed; stories of "Pop Star's Secret Wife" became meaningless rather than sensational simply because there were so many such stories, and, anyway, the fans didn't much care. But that wasn't the case in 1965, when Tom Jones erupted. Then the feeling, at best, was that wives were not exactly helpful in boosting a teen-appeal career.

And Tom most definitely was married—to a child-hood sweetheart, Melinda, known as Linda. They were both only sixteen when they were married. Tom, born in Treforrest, met the eleven-year-old Linda when his family moved to Pontypridd, to a terraced house just round the corner from Linda's. Their mothers were friendly, and there were frequent family get-togethers.

40

Women and a Wife

In a rare interview Linda recalled how she was invited to a party when Tom's sister Freda became engaged. Even then, Linda recalled, Tom was determined to be the star of the show and he sang his favorite song, "Ghost Riders in the Sky," rapping out the rhythm with complete authority. Linda was most impressed. And she continued to encourage Tom when he bought himself a cheap guitar and set out on that lonely search for recognition round the local clubs. Her support meant a lot to Tom. Gradually their boy-girl friendship developed into love. Certainly it was no surprise to the neighbors when they got married, for neighbors in Pontypridd tended to know everything that was going on.

Times were hard for both of them when Tom moved to London to look for his slice of fame and fortune. He found the streets were paved not with gold but with concrete, and concrete was hard on the feet as one traipsed from audition to audition, from interview to pointless, boring interview. Linda, with Mark to look after, lived at her parents' home, was kept busy, but there was little money. Tom borrowed from Gordon Mills and sent what he could back home, but life was a struggle.

Tom has often said that his marriage is a good one just because he doesn't believe in equal rights for women. He says that the man has to be the boss all the time and should take the lead and let the woman follow. He's really convinced, in his own mind, that this superior-inferior relationship is the true basis for making a marriage work.

An understanding of Tom's thinking about marriage explains why he felt so low during his early bad spell in London: for just that once his principle of man's being boss had broken down; his wife had had to find a part-time job because her husband couldn't support her.

Tom's relationship with his son has been consistently good, even though they are separated for long periods of each year. Tom has said that he brings the boy into major discussions at home, even over some of his projected million-dollar show business deals. "The lad is interested in my job," he says. "Maybe one day I'd like to see him in show business, because he knows a lot about pop music, certainly knows what is good and what's bad. If he can't sing or act, then perhaps he could go into the management side of the business."

Tom told one reporter that he felt he and his son were more like brothers. Even so, he stressed, he could never be weak with the boy. He took his responsibilities seriously and laid down the law whenever necessary.

Tom's and Linda's was, and is, a teenage marriage that really worked. Tom, however, had been an extremely old sixteen, and he felt that marriage was a great help in making him a complete man. He accepted his responsibilities manfully, realizing he couldn't just drift along anymore, and was upset only because lack of money at first meant he couldn't live up to his own principles: that a man must always look after his wife and child. Moreover, when Linda had to take a job while Tom was in London, some of the Welsh townspeople were not amused. They got the impression, wrong, as

42

it happened, that Tom was ducking out on his responsibilities and just leading some wild playboy life up in the big city.

Not long after Linda and Mark moved to London to join Tom, news of their marriage got out. There had been no really deliberate policy to hide his family; fortunately, nobody had bothered to ask. Linda has said she was worried when the story broke because pop music was in that period when fans could turn very petty if they thought they were being deliberately misled over a star's private life.

The letters poured in. Some fans couldn't hide their disappointment that the new hero figure had a heroine of his own. The reaction was inevitable. Here was a real he-man hunk, new to the pop headlines, and there he was—married. Happily married, which somehow made it worse.

Tom, as one would expect, faced the new situation characteristically. In one interview he said: "A big part of life itself is sex. If you are a man, you should try and show yourself a man, and the same goes for a woman. As far as the girls in my working life are concerned, my wife knows it is my business. But when she first came to London, it took a bit of time for her to get used to it.

"I had to explain it to her then. But I don't have to anymore. We've been together now for so long that we can talk about things more openly than if we had been married only recently. I'm glad I got married when I did. Now I wouldn't know whether a girl wanted me as a person or for what I am."

And Linda said: "When Tom really hit the top of the charts, I began to get this burning feeling inside. It's just nature, isn't it? How do you think it makes me feel, seeing all those other women setting their caps at Tom?"

Tom's success meant that life was turned upside down for Linda, and she often admitted that she felt insecure and jealous. As she explained it: "They told Tom to say he wasn't married at first, but the subject didn't really come up. But it made me feel so nervous. I sometimes had this feeling that I really shouldn't be there at all. That I didn't really belong to his new world."

On another occasion she said: "It was a terrible thing to be told to stay hidden, to sort of disappear. I just used to shut myself in a room when people came. It's better now, of course, now that people know of our family life."

Apart from a few interviews early in Tom's career, Linda has kept in the background simply because she prefers it that way. She has come to appreciate that Tom's appeal is largely for other women, and, when success arrived, she never much enjoyed watching him work his magic onstage. For that magic still rubbed off on her, even after twelve or thirteen years, and her own feelings, she realized, were being duplicated and multiplied in hundreds of hearts in hundreds of audiences. That wasn't easy to take. So Linda took the less difficult way out. Sometimes she'd travel to meet Tom in different parts of the world, just for a few days, but mostly she was happy to stay at home and wait for the daily phone call from the family's breadwinner.

44

Women and a Wife

Later, at the peak of his popularity in the United States, Tom was to reiterate his views on man's being essentially the dominant character in any family organization. Not entirely a popular point of view to propagate in U.S. society!

There was a woman, an ordinary American woman, whose husband had died, suddenly and tragically. This woman said that her immediate feeling was of nothingness, of a void, of having nothing left to live for. She had thought of ending her sorrow, once and for all. All that occupied her was picking out the actual means of committing suicide. And then, she said, there was Tom Jones. She said his music—his songs—had helped her pull herself together so that she felt able once more to face an unhelpful world.

Tom was pleased at the compliment. But he repeated his views: "I think a woman's job is to serve her man. But men have let women go too far. They give them equal rights and I don't believe in that. You talk to career women today and they say: 'How can I listen to HIM? I must do my own thing because I have no faith in him.' But if a man is a man, a real man, then his woman will want to depend on him. When a woman goes with a guy, she sees something in him. It's not just a sexual need, but something in his character she likes and she gives herself.

"A man will take any girl to bed, but it has nothing to do with any attraction for her or his love for his wife. A woman may like to think she is equal, but she's not, because when she loves her man, she'll be faithful to him. You see, a woman's love for a man is greater than a man's love for a woman."

45

Tom, then, it is clear, after a hesitant start had little difficulty in getting over the problems of having a wife and son. Partly this was the result of a change in the makeup of his audience. In the early stages his fans were mostly teenagers, lapping up his vocal virility after the comparative whisperings of some of the other Top Twenty merchants. Later the average age of his fan following went up substantially. When he moved into the tuxedo belt, out of the jeans-and-boots scene, he was getting into a part of show business where a wife in the wings was no trouble at all.

One look at Tom and there was no doubting his manliness. And there were doubts galore about others in the pop world. That Tom had married as a very young stud, had raised a son—well, to the older woman that was just fine. They still got vicarious kicks out of mental images involving the physical Tom, but the difference was that they *knew* it would be good if their dreams came true.

Being married, somehow, just set the seal on his extreme manliness. It was further proof that he was superconfident in his own masculinity.

Yet there was much evidence that Tom really was a home-loving boy, despite his rowdier moments as a kid. His parents, unbelievably proud of how he'd become a star, are open-faced, friendly people. As their home, first in Wales and later in London, became something of a shrine for the fans, they were always ready with a hospitable cup of tea and friendly reminiscences about their famous son. For instance, when two fans traveled down from Birmingham to London, armed with

gifts for Mr. and Mrs. Woodward, they got on so well
with Tom's folks that they stayed all day.

When Tom first moved to London, his parents missed
him badly. As they put it once: "He always came to see
us when he was in Wales, even after he got married,
but later on it got difficult. So many relations and
friends he had to meet, and so little time to get to Wales,
and he ended up with less time to spend with any of us.
But we knew he'd never really change, no matter how
big he became as a singer. He has this strength of character, you see. And even when he handed over his old
house to us, it was all done without any kind of show.
He just said to us how he knew we'd always liked the
place and so it was ours to keep."

Mind you, said Tom's father, it took a lot of persuasion for them to move away from Pontypridd. He'd been
working in the coal mines for forty years and there
were eight more years to go before he could settle down
to retirement. He said: "After all that time, you get set
in your ways. You just don't know any other way of
living. I was happy enough in the mine, I suppose, and
it didn't worry me that Tom just didn't want to follow
me in the same job.

"He had this talent for singing, so I thought why the
hell shouldn't he use it. The mining life, with all the
comradeship, was fine for me, but I was much happier
that Tom made up his own mind what to do with his
life."

Tom's parents soon adjusted to the new way of life,
though. Not so long after Tom made it big, they were
living in Paul Newman's house in Bel Air, Los Angeles,

and thoroughly enjoying soaking up the luxury of living in film star surroundings.

True in a way to his own beliefs about the basic inequality of women, Tom really idolized his father. Asked what he'd learned from his dad, he said the main thing was that he'd always been a real man: making his own decisions and fighting his own battles and letting nobody put him down. When the Jones family went on holiday, for example, his dad would install Tom, his sister, and mother on the beach and then go off for a beer drinking session on his own if he felt like it. Not a popular move with most wives, a sort of revolt against the togetherness of a family holiday, but Tom explained: "My dad just refused to be hen-pecked."

Like father, like son: an old adage but true enough in Tom's own life. And nobody can doubt that his own son, Mark, will grow up capable of standing on his own two feet, standing up for his own rights.

Tom's closely knit family ties have been no hindrance to his rise to fame as a sex-image song seller. So many times, a pop career has been wrecked because of a too possessive wife. Tom established right away that he was going to run the show his own way and that way was to be boss, right from the start.

5　One Hit Is Not Success

Tom Jones took quite well to the round of cocktail parties and interviews, and the reporters and photographers took well to him. He had a no-nonsense sort of image: proud of his roots yet glad to have broken away and given himself a chance to express himself creatively, still capable of grinning mockingly at the jumped-up importance placed on interviews with the teen-appeal pop magazines.

It took a special kind of personality and character to cope. The questions, if any are actually asked at these press get-togethers, are, in the main, trivial. "Tom, what do you eat for breakfast?" "Eggs and bacon." Eyebrows unaccountably rise and the reply is gushingly thankful. "Oooh, good—yes, fine—that's great, Tom, thanks."

Maybe a girl reporter from a fan magazine plunges in with, "What do you wear in bed, Tom? Pajamas . . .

maybe you sleep in the raw?" Whatever he answered produced a simper or a sigh. But there had to be this feeding of futile facts because the teenage magazine field is crowded, and the ones who don't get the titillating tidbits go out of business.

Some pop stars fired off fatuous answers by way of showing their resentment. It would have been easy for Tom to do just that. But, instead, he impressed the writers, even those more interested in what made him tick musically, with his modesty and his offstage quietness.

Those who hadn't actually seen him in action by early 1965 had certainly heard of his ultraviolent stage act and many half expected him to be a tearaway rocker who answered mostly in grunts and monosyllables. Tom, however, genuinely tried to be helpful, tactful, diplomatic.

He had, anyway, an ability to get on with other men. He wore some pretty way-out clothes, but it was easy to see that there wasn't anything soft about him. "I'd rather have him on my side than against me," was the attitude. And the women journalists fell for the direct gaze, the tough profile, the battered nose, the broad shoulders, the quick smile, and the impression he'd picked up early that there was only one woman in the world—the one asking a question at that very moment. Of course, he got bored at the endless round of questions. But he was realist enough to know that most publicity was good publicity.

Anybody facing a barrage of pop-type questions soon gets to know the score. Take it seriously, but, for goodness sake, don't get your stories mixed up. If you say you like rum and Coke, then stick to it, because the facts culled from those first interviews will be dug up out of cuttings files for years and years to come.

The Beatles, not so long before, had learned the hard way that it didn't pay to be too flippant. Paul McCartney projected an insatiable enthusiasm for processed-cheese slices and was inundated with cartons of a food that he didn't really like much at all. And when the group as a whole said they liked jelly beans they were greeted onstage by barrages of hard-hurled candies— and even a jelly bean can hurt if flung with accuracy and speed.

And if Tom was a bit naive in the ways of pop projection, it rarely showed through. As "It's Not Unusual" raced up the Top Twenty ratings, he still mixed with his musician friends, downing his pints of beer with experience and smoking more than enough cigarettes to keep that rough edge to his voice.

He'd found himself caught up in the full helter-skelter pace of pop music. His record was being played all the time on radio, blaring out from jukeboxes along with the Presley platters and the Beatles' hits. It took time to adjust. As he said at the time: "When I'm in a pub and my record comes on, I have to watch myself or I feel like getting up and telling everybody that it's me and I'm here."

In the background, though, there was always that fear that he'd wind up as a one-hit wonder—a frightening thought to a new star. At the same time, there was plenty of evidence that Tom really had what it takes to stay at the top. For example, he was given some dates on a tour with Cilla Black, taking over on some of the shows from P. J. Proby, then a big star.

This was a major break for a lad who had previously played only to Welsh audiences. It also had an ironic touch; for P. J. Proby, an American with a knack of hitting the headlines, was a performer in much the same mold as Tom. He was violent, sexy, rugged, brilliant, too, though constantly involved in rows with managements, journalists, record companies. Eventually, Proby was to disappear from the pop-topping scene. Most who studied his work felt he had the ability to be a complete international star, but his career was studded with so much hell raising that in the end the verdict was: A shame, but he should have kept his mouth shut except for singing—and now it's too late.

The history of pop music shows that it's not only the no-hopers and no-talents who are quickly buried in the graveyard of failed ambition. There were also many great performers who just couldn't get the one big breakthrough and in the end had to be written off, even by their most enthusiastic fans.

Tom sold his own brand of sexiness around the one-nighter tour, and gradually the fatuous personal questions were dropped. Writers became interested in what really made him stand out from the crowd. They wanted to know how he maintained, night after night, his almost savage attacks on captive-but-happy audiences.

Tom explained it this way to the London *Daily Mail*:

"I just get it across that I'm alive. I've got to be able to grab 'em and not let go . . . this is me, singing, you see. I've got to get everything across. All of it, the emotion, the sex, the power, the heartbeat and the bloodstream is all theirs for the taking. You see, man, all the others, the other singers back to the Marty Wildes, the Billy Furys and the P. J. Probys are really only imitations of Elvis Presley. I don't go for them at all."

But he agreed that he would go on producing his own fair share of pelvic gyrations. He said: "But the words, you see, don't mean so much unless the body gets into the act. Al Jolson got down on his knees, Danny Kaye makes it with his hips, the best coloured singers move, man, move; I admit I shove it about a bit, but I don't spell it out like Proby. It's the emotion that triggers off the body—I just let it go."

Put like that, there didn't seem much malice afore-thought in the way he sold sex appeal in near-fatal doses. But Elvis Presley's own career had been threatened in the early days when outraged sections of the community in the United States wanted him banned for life. Tom had followed, admired, and respected Elvis Presley. He knew the Presley history.

The Presley problems were well known. There was the Rev. Carl E. Elgena, pastor of a Baptist church in Des Moines, Iowa, who said: "Elvis Presley is morally insane. The spirit of Presleyism has taken down all the bars and standards, and we're now living in a day of jellyfish morality."

In Bridgeport, Connecticut, five teenage boys were

53

arrested on robbery charges. They said they stole to finance a trip to an Elvis Presley show. The District Attorney said: "Elvis Presley is an inspiration for low IQ hoodlums and ought to be entertaining in the State Reformatory."

Elvis, asked if he felt that his performances could contribute to juvenile delinquency, said: "If I thought that was true, sir, I would quit and go back to driving a truck. I wouldn't do anything to hurt anybody, sir. Money doesn't mean anything to me. It's this business I love."

Elvis learned to cope with the criticism in a self-assured but likable way, and admitted being hurt by remarks like those of Harold Fellows, president of the National Association of Radio and Television Broadcasters, who said: "Elvis Presley is one of the biggest problems we have got today . . . a problem of American Society. Much too many are going crazy about Presley. The better job people do in the field of religion, the sooner Presley will go."

Of course, Elvis never did go.

All this was years before Tom arrived to energize a pop scene that desperately needed a transfusion of real red blood. But there were criticisms of his style, nevertheless, and the usual bigoted opinions, mostly from people who had never seen Tom Jones in action and were barely aware of what he was getting at with the chart-topping "It's Not Unusual."

Critics made efforts to play up a major feud between Tom Jones and P. J. Proby, and, predictably, the first

Grass turns gold for Tom.

Rex Features Ltd. Photo by David Magnus

Getting to know London.

After his first hit, "It's Not Unusual."

Right: Stepping out with Walk on By—a new status symbol for Tom in 1967.

Below: *Melody Maker* pop awards winners in 1966.

Above: Tom celebrating with his parents, November, 1967.

Below: Tom and his ocean-going yacht—another status symbol.

The Joneses move into their new Sunbury house.

Keystone Press Agency Ltd.

Above: Tom with two of his millions of fans.

Below: Tom congratulates Sandie Shaw on her success with "Puppet on a String."

Pictorial Press Ltd.

punches were slung from Proby's corner when Proby implied that Tom was copying the Proby style and that he could never be a real sex symbol. In reply, Tom, mustering maximum dignity though he was near blowing up inside, said: "I am just what I am. I have never tried to be what is popularly conceived as a modern sex symbol. Take a look at these sideburns and the curly hair, brushed back. Do you see any sign of the idol with a fringe and velvet pants [a direct dig at Proby]. I was singing the same kind of songs, dressed as I am now, when Proby was still back in America. I don't copy anybody, least of all Proby."

And in the same "Question Time" feature in *New Musical Express*, Tom said he did not really like Proby as an artist. "I respect his voice and like his sound. But not his style. I think it would be a good idea if we met before either of us says anything else in print about the other."

But Proby, whose velvet pants "unaccountably" split, top to bottom, during a concert appearance (an incident that led to his being banned from many theaters and cinemas in Britain), continued "a-fussin' and a-feudin'," constantly saying he'd take on Tom in a singing battle, leaving the winner to be selected by the audience.

Tom, whose sole gimmick was a rabbit's foot attached to his belt and who was as quietly inclined as Proby was egotistical in his confidence, wouldn't be drawn. He hadn't spent years learning to project his voice in song only to have his first taste of pop stardom wrecked by some crazy mixed-up effort at headline grabbing. Besides, Gordon Mills would never have let him get involved.

What's more, Tom was impressively realistic about the success of that first record. He owned that it was the quality of the song and the arrangement that had pushed it into the charts. "After all," he said, "nobody knew much about Tom Jones and most everybody thought it was my first record." He paid tribute to the Ivy League, three singers who helped him out on the backing, and to Gordon Mills and Les Reed, who wrote the song, and to Les Reed for arranging it. "Without them," he said stolidly, "I'd still be nowhere."

After "It's Not Unusual," Tom was out on his own, having to prove his own quality and temperament, pushed into the nerve-wracking atmosphere of the television studios. Before the record, Tom had made one television appearance, on "Donald Peers Presents," a showcase for little-known talent, and he'd talked to Peers about the struggles that a singer has in breaking through.

Peers knew all about that. For a long time he had been the glamour-boy hero of the housewives, capable of packing such giant venues like the Royal Albert Hall with his straight, square, bouncy style of singing romantic, schmaltzy pop songs. A podgy, gentle sort of man, Peers had been just about the most unlikely swoon merchant of all time. His success was, in the pre-beat group days, nothing short of sensational. In the end, his popularity faded as tastes changed, and thereafter Donald was to have only occasional moments of success in the recording world. Peers and Jones had much to talk about.

After his first success Tom Jones listened and learned, and he settled into the routine of appearing on the top pop television shows. His best performances were given on "Ready, Steady, Go" because there he had a live audience urging him on through his mixture of vocal and physical gymnastics. Obviously he responded best in front of an audience. He'd already learned that he could control the emotions and feelings of large numbers of people by a judicious wiggle, or a frantic yip and holler. But when there was no audience, only a handful of cameramen and technicians, all too busy to get caught up in the fury of a Tom Jones song—well, he found it harder to find top gear.

And Tom was already talking of his new ambition: he wanted to become a truly international figure. Those close to pop music had heard it all before. A singer makes a single hit record and then starts talking of world domination. But Tom at least had a secret weapon—manager Gordon Mills, who knew instinctively that the United States was where the big money lay, and so he quietly got on with his plans to promote Tom into one of the very few British entertainers to create real impact in the United States.

First, though, there was the problem of finding a song with sufficient impact to be a worthwhile follow-up to "It's Not Unusual." Without the constant plugging of a second hit record, the name of Tom Jones could have faded. He would have been sent back to the obscurity of the Welsh valleys.

6   The First U.S. Visit

Though he'd never been short of energy, Tom Jones found the panic-station rush of being top of the charts took more out of him than he'd expected. Suddenly, everybody wanted to know him, and everybody wanted to show him off as a valuable status symbol at parties and receptions.

He took it very well. His hobbies went by the board as he leaped from conference to meeting. He had little time to play through his collection of Jerry Lee Lewis records. "I could listen to him all night," he said. "Just curl up in a big chair and lose myself in his music." Even pop idols have pop idols, and Tom told people how part of his stage act had been inspired by the American rock and roller.

Tom had little time, either, for his sketching. He worked well, in pencil most of the time, and drew landscapes, portraits, more or less anything that took his

59

fancy. But sketching takes time, and Tom was short of time. He'd maybe watch television and take in the occasional Western movie, but most of the time he was on the move.

Apart from the business side, he wanted to set up a home of his own in London, so that his wife and son could join him. Inevitably, he spent a small fortune on phone calls back home, passing on news of the latest developments in what was already a sensational rise to fame.

It takes enormous physical fitness to cope with the rigors of a star's life. Tom had a good sporting background and had always liked to keep himself in trim. At high school he'd played Rugby football for the school team and occasionally turned out in soccer matches. Cricket bored him because it was too slow, and he preferred to be where the action was. He'd worked out at a local boxing club with friends. This active childhood and youth helped enormously when it came to meeting the great strain of appearing in a different venue each night, often not having time to grab more than a sandwich beforehand.

He went swimming, sometimes, when there was a break in the schedule, but it was mostly a life of sheer hard work. Tom missed out badly on his sleep, and this was one of the biggest problems he had to face. "I hate getting up early in the morning," he said. "And I hate having to shave at that unearthly hour. So I take an electric razor round with me, only to find that most dressing rooms don't have the right sort of plug."

A trivial point, yes, but the sort of thing that leads to

extreme irritability when a new star is on the way up and wants everything to fall into place so he can put on a perfect show. Tom suffered a rash of flat tires, too, which caused delays on the way to engagements. It was hard persuading managements that it really was an accident, because they'd heard all the excuses before from erratic, unreliable beat groups. Tom wanted desperately to prove his reliability and punctuality and became very upset when plain bad luck got in the way of his schedule.

Still, he felt he was at long last on the way to financial security. Some people have said that with one hit record by itself you can really hit the jackpot. It doesn't quite work out like that. However, Tom was able to go ahead with plans to build a $17,000 house at Shepperton, no mansion even by English standards, but a place in the country, close enough to London, that also guaranteed a certain measure of seclusion.

Melody Maker, a long-established music-business weekly, tried to analyze just what a gigantic hit record would mean to Tom. It worked out at maybe $120,000, including all the personal appearances and increased fees associated with a hit record. Tom told Chris Welch, "I want to keep my personal spending down but there are a lot more expenses now. I bought a new van for my backing group, which I've augmented by three musicians, and I have to have my own personal road manager." Even after the expenses Tom was still way ahead. His earning power had been about $100 a night for the group and himself. With a hit record, it was up around the $700-a-night mark.

According to Tom: "One of the biggest effects is that success gives you more confidence in your work. Before, the group was getting fed up and disillusioned, but now we all have a contented feeling. You immediately get more money. Now I can buy better suits—and I'm buying dozens of shirts for stage wear. Why I even snatched a few days' holiday in Juan-les-Pins with my wife—and I'd never have even thought of that before." Previously it would have taken a year of hard saving to get away for a holiday abroad.

The one hit had other effects, too. Tom said: "On the work level, the impact is all that much greater. In the old days, I had to reckon on doing three or four songs in order to get the audience really with me. Now it is more or less instantaneous. The crowds have come to expect more, but that's all right with me, because I feel I have to give more and have more to give."

But if Tom Jones had made a good beginning, it was just that—a beginning. Never for a moment did Gordon or Tom falter in their view that the first $100,000 was only the start of the story. But a career that moves so fast is bound to have some setbacks. Tom felt at the time that a "blast from the past" in the form of a record produced by him some two years earlier, in 1963, could do his career a lot of harm.

We've already seen that Tom's "official" recording career started with the flop "Chills and Fever," but obviously a man of Tom's experience had been in recording studios before. In fact, as Tommy Scott, along with the Senators, Tom Jones had spent some time in bizarre studios run by Joe Meek, in north London. Joe, now dead, set up his equipment in his apartment and found that some very commercial pop sounds could be created by the echo effects that came from recording in his bathroom. His biggest hit, by far, was to be "Telstar," sung by the Tornados, a record that sold more than five million copies around the world. It was an insidious, organ-dominated instrumental that tied in topically with the first telecommunications satellite.

Joe, ever an optimist, was always on the lookout for real talent. It was said that he never turned away a young hopeful, and if the talent was really there, he spared no efforts to launch a kid into the big time. Tom and the Senators arrived from Wales and cut seven tracks during a session with Joe Meek. One of the songs recorded was "Little Lonely One." Joe was ostensibly pleased with the result and said he would see that it was released.

Tom and the boys returned to Wales but heard nothing more about it. As far as they were concerned, it was just another of the disappointments that cropped up regularly in their erratic search for fame. Promises, promises—always promises. Few people ever did anything to make them come true.

Eventually there was a dispute between Tom and the Senators and Joe, and in the end the boys got their contract back. Later came the contract with Decca, but the tapes of that original session were still held by Joe. Perhaps it is not surprising that he decided to cash in on Tom's new star status. At any rate, "Little Lonely One" came out in May, 1965, on the Parlophone label, hot on the heels of Tom's "official," completely up-to-date follow-up single: "Once Upon a Time."

Arguments still rage in the record industry about the

moral aspects of releasing old material to coincide with a sudden jump to fame of an artist. Certainly there are two completely opposite points of view.

Many artists go from record company to record company, from label to label, searching for the right sort of atmosphere and guidance to make a hit record. The companies have to invest money in those sessions and in producing the tapes and records. In fairness, it can be argued that they have a right to try to get their money back. Consequently, if an artist goes elsewhere and becomes a big name, they feel they have the right to bring out material available to them under an original copyright.

However, the "old" company never bothers to state clearly in the advertising material that theirs is an old recording: that would be a form of business suicide, obviously. So the old material can come out, competing confusingly with a genuine follow-up. And it was that lack of information on the label of "Little Lonely One" that upset Tom Jones at the time. About "Little Lonely One" he said: "It all happened two years ago and I think that it's a dated sound and I want to disassociate myself from what is on that record. Tastes have changed a lot since it was made and I think it only confuses the general public."

Predictably, Joe Meek hit back. He said that he felt it was a good record and that Tom should be "proud" of having it out on the market. It all added up to a problem that has been faced by many of the biggest names in pop, and Tom was simply unlucky having to meet it head-on so early in his career. In the end, he had the last laugh, because while he ignored the old track on his television appearances and radio guest spots, "Once Upon a Time" was an easy-moving hit.

Still, if "Little Lonely One" was an arguable setback for Tom, the demand for him in the United States most certainly was not. "It's Not Unusual" raced up the U.S. charts, and he flew out with Gordon Mills for intensive promotional work on it. He was an instant smash hit. Appearing on the highly rated, networked, Ed Sullivan Show, he opened and closed the production, and the station switchboards were jammed with callers wanting to know more about the young British star who clearly had put honest sex back into show business. Tom swirled his hips, jerked his arms, sold every available muscle in his body. And the Negro quality of his voice amazed even top black stars such as Mary Wells, who watched Tom explode on a Murray the K production.

Mary and many others had heard Tom's hard sell of "Unusual" on radio, especially on some of the stations that played virtually all black-artist records. And it wasn't until the publicity pictures were splashed all over the United States that people realized he was a white man, but a white man singing with every ounce of feeling normally associated with the black man's rhythm and blues.

The black reaction to his singing was flattering to Tom Jones, who had so much personal regard for black artists such as Solomon Burke and Otis Redding, not to forget the more ballady approach of Brook Benton. And he was much impressed by the care with which he was presented on U.S. television. He enjoyed taping shows in advance because the process always allowed time to go back and correct mistakes. The hit-or-miss aspect of the live performance appealed to the gambler in him, but this was his chance for a takeover in U.S. show business, and he wanted to make sure that everything was completely right on the night. Live audiences turned him on, but this time he was so excited by the potential that he had no need of an audience.

One U.S. columnist said that he couldn't remember a more exciting performance from any singer since the days of Elvis Presley. And here again, there was a link.

When Elvis first appeared on national television networks in the United States, it was decreed that if he simply couldn't, or wouldn't, keep his whirling and swiveling pelvis reasonably still, cameramen would be instructed to shoot him only from the waist up. Similar mutterings were heard on the set of the Ed Sullivan Show. But in the end, all of Tom was presented for national edification and education, and the result was incredible.

Tom's big record in the United States was "What's New, Pussycat," which was released soon afterward in Britain where, despite some reservations from Tom himself, it was a very big seller.

"What's New, Pussycat" was a Burt Bacharach song, written for a movie, with Tom singing it on the actual film soundtrack. Tom's reasons for being doubtful about the qualities of the song are a little obscure. What he said was: "I honestly thought it might have been a temporary end of the road for me on disc . . . it just didn't seem completely right for me at that stage of my career."

The First U.S. Visit

"What's New, Pussycat" was a change of style for Bacharach, too, with the hurdy-gurdy sounds and the offbeat sound effects, and he spent a lot of time both writing and producing Tom in the studio. The Jones boy was most grateful for the advice and encouragement from the U.S. composer.

That Burt and Tom should get on well was only to be expected. Both are very much men's men. Burt, as a kid, had been a fanatical sportsman; his mother once said she doubted whether he'd have ever learned to read or write if it had not been for his sudden craze to learn to play piano. Burt went on to become one of the most successful composers in popular music, along with his collaborator, Hal David, and he also had a big share in the disc development of Tom Jones.

During the summer of 1965 Tom literally roared across the United States. There was a tour with the Dick Clark "Caravan of Stars," all the top television dates, and a flying visit to Bermuda to appear at the Forty Thieves Club. For ten weeks and more, Tom stretched himself to the limit of his endurance. That so-called idle chat of wanting to become an international star was bearing fruit much quicker than anybody, except maybe Gordon Mills, could have expected.

Tom missed his family, his friends, and his backing group. The Squires did not make the trip, and Tom had trouble finding drummers who could really put down a helluva beat and urge on the singer. He was playing to younger audiences in the United States in 1965 than he does today, and there were warnings that he would have to cut down on some of his stage movements. But taming Tom was very much like trying to tame a tiger. It took courage to argue with him that he was being suggestive when all the time he felt he was just doing what came naturally.

At the Brooklyn Fox theater, Tom appeared in front of an all-black audience, giving one of his most uninhibited performances ever. As he talked about his acceptance by these fans, who normally feel lukewarm toward white entertainers, the pride showed through.

At the famed Apollo Theater in Harlem, Tom was virtually the only white man in the building. Chuck Jackson hailed him on stage as "the great British star who sings 'What's New, Pussycat'," and Tom received a great reception.

Everything was going well. Tom was making friends all around with Americans who were impressed with his offbeat mixture of toughness and modesty. His progress was viewed with a mixture of awe and bemusement. One hit record . . . off to America . . . superstar . . . another hit record. All in very much less than a year. And if Tom was thousands of miles away, news of his progress still reached home.

In the *Melody Maker* popularity poll, published in September, 1965, he came in fifth place in the British section of the top singer category. He was beaten by Cliff Richard, Donovan, Mick Jagger, and John Lennon. But it's interesting to note that he was highest of all the new entries to the category, and he defeated Billy Fury and Eric Burdon (of the Animals). In tenth place was P. J. Proby, the man who had had most to say against Tom's emergence on the pop scene. "It's Not Unusual" was placed in the top ten vocal records of the year, and Tom also ended in fourth place in the "Brightest Hope for 1966" department.

There had been more dominating first appearances in a popularity poll. But it should be remembered that Tom's impact time in Britain had been almost short compared with the amount of exposure he had received in America.

What was obvious was that Tom was well away from the danger of being a short-term star, a one-hit wonder. And it was equally clear that he was beginning to appeal to all age groups and sections. He was screamed at by the teenagers, but he was also creating alarmingly extreme outbreaks of starry-eyedness among the matrons, and the males who happened to like a good song, well sung, warmed to him because he wasn't like the hairy pop groups mushrooming on both sides of the Atlantic.

As he barnstormed around the United States, Tom was understandably wide-eyed and tired eyed. He liked the people because they weren't reserved, and he enjoyed answering their questions about where he came from and what he liked about America. As disc jockey Paul Drew, one of the top programmers in the States, said, "We took to Tom because he was so obviously anxious to be friendly. Some of the best things in pop were coming from Britain, but here was a guy who really sang well and packed guts into his voice."

There was an extra special helping of guts and vitality on Tom's first album, released in Britain in May. Called simply *Along Came Jones* and released in the United States as *It's Not Unusual*, it was immediately

69

hailed as one of the best debut albums of all time. This was another vital hurdle cleared. Already it was apparent that Tom's long-term buildup would not be made on the strength of singles alone.

In pop music, a single is a short-arm stab. In recent years, the sales of singles have dropped and the album market has extended. But not everybody who makes a hit single has the ability to extend entertainment over the forty minutes or so of an album. Tom, already well into the cabaret field by the end of 1965, had to produce the goods over a lengthy stage act. This album showed how far he'd progressed, and it is worth including all the titles, just to show the range of his versatility: "I've Got a Heart," "It Takes a Worried Man," "Skye Boat Song," "Once Upon a Time," "Memphis, Tennessee," "Whatcha Gonna Do," "I Need Your Loving," "It's Not Unusual," "Autumn Leaves," "The Rose," "If You Need Me," "Some Other Guy," "Endlessly," "It's Just a Matter of Time," "Spanish Harlem," "When the World Was Beautiful." ("I've Got a Heart" and "The Rose" were omitted from the U.S. version.)

A Welshman singing a Scottish song, and turning the whole thing inside out in the process; a Welshman singing a Negro's original; a Welshman fitting his talents into a Latin-American setting. *Along Came Jones* had to be, and was, a massive seller. It also helped to bridge the gap while Tom was in the United States undertaking his one-man invasion of pop music.

Meanwhile, Tom, as if he couldn't trust his good fortune and skill, remained, as the buildup plowed remorselessly on, a slightly superstitious star who kept all the rabbits' feet, emblems of good luck, sent him by his fans, in a big box. If, as happened, he occasionally had a crucifix torn from around his neck as a souvenir, he received many replacements once the news of his loss got around. Handfuls of hair weren't so easy to replace. "Man, that hurts—it really hurts," he'd say after a really vicious mugging by the more determined fans.

By the end of 1965 every Tom Jones record was given the treatment it deserved. While "Unusual" had miraculously passed almost unnoticed at the time of release, he was now being hailed for each single. As top disc reviewer Penny Valentine said of one release: "This is not a record. This is a record and a half. I have never, in my life, heard anyone put so much voice on one 45 rpm."

That record was "With These Hands," a revival of an oldie that had been a hit for Billy Eckstine and others, that seared the summer. "With These Hands" was a complete change from Tom's earlier records, with lots of piano, a battery of strings. Clearly, he had not only created a well-nigh unassailable position for himself in the disc world, but he'd gained the confidence to ring the changes on his material. Too often, Gordon Mills, in his management role, knew, an artist had dropped out of favor simply by sticking to the same kind of song in the same kind of orchestral setting.

"With These Hands" found its way into the hands of Elvis Presley, who immediately rated it one of his all-time favorites. And long before the end of 1965, there was a "summit meeting" of America's long-time pop leader and Britain's new boy. Tom went along to

71

watch Elvis filming in Hollywood. There was a gap in the shooting and the two were introduced and Elvis paid Tom the compliment of singing a few bars of "With These Hands," to prove he knew what it was all about. The pop world is comparatively small—the two singing giants even exchanged a few personal reminiscences about . . . P. J. Proby!

Tom, still excited about the meeting, said upon his return to Britain: "It wasn't a put-up job. The meeting went on for about half-an-hour and honest! you'd never realize that guy was *the* Elvis Presley. A very nice character and just meeting him took me back to the days when I collected every record he made and liked all of them."

But there were rumblings of discontent among Tom's fans in Britain. They heard his records daily on radio, but there wasn't much hard news coming back from the United States, except the fact that Tom was doing well. Pitfalls crop up everywhere, but it is worth remembering that a British artist who stays away too long can wreck his chances of long-time support from his own public.

So Tom returned, eventually, and said, "Love America and dig the people. But in Britain I feel I'm really in the centre of the music business. America is so large, you tend to feel you're on the outside looking in. British groups, especially the guys with long hair, are doing well in the States, but I realise so much that I owe a great deal to the fans who have supported me in Britain. Believe me, I have a heck of a lot to be grateful for."

7 A Period of Retrenchment

In studying any important pop music career, it is apparent that there are moments of total triumph followed by periods where the trend is downward and the outlook is not so bright. Looked at in retrospect, and comparing it with other times, the career of Tom Jones had its most "down" period in 1966. He worked hard and worked well. But there were feelings of anticlimax, particularly viewed in the light of what had gone on in the previous twelve months.

Tom was back from the United States and rarin' to go, but some of his singles failed to make the expected impact. "This and That" was one that had weak impact, and "Stop Breaking My Heart" didn't do much for his fans' peace of mind. Yet he was earning very big money in clubs and theaters, was happily settled into his new home, and was in the throes of being regarded as something very much more than "just" a recording artist.

The honors were still heaped upon him, though, back home in Wales. He was made President of the Woodrow Social Club—the place he'd got to know well as a lowly paid singer years before. It was just an extra surprise for Tom when he went home at Christmas and was hailed as the conquering hero by the local town councilors and dignitaries. Tom enjoyed this brief spell at home. He liked going for a pint with the neighbors, often with his parents and family, and he appreciated the way the good folk of Pontypridd didn't treat him as "somebody from outer space."

They'd greet him, shake him by the hand, buy him a pint of beer, but not take it any further. True, some of them imagined he'd probably developed a very big head indeed, what with mixing with all those film stars and having all that success, but most of them felt he was destined to be a star, anyway. Even when he was singing for just a few cents a show they regarded him as a star-in-the-making.

The local kids gawked at his big cars when he made a big trip home. And in the bar of the Wheatsheaf public house, Tom talked mostly about his cars, or his family, almost everything but the scenes he'd experienced in the United States. The point is that Tom Jones was still Tommy Woodward at heart, a local boy with a lot of friends, and the friends wanted to make him feel relaxed when he did get to see the green, green grass of his own home.

Tom appreciated their thoughtfulness, but he didn't have the time to stay long. From Wales, to London, to Australia. True, his recording of "Goldfinger" was not exactly burning up the charts, but Australia offered a completely new challenge. He took the Squires with him, and they enjoyed five weeks in the sunshine, swimming a little and always working a lot. Tom packed his American lightweight suits and really settled down to the tour. He had Herman's Hermits on the bill with him, which was a fair guarantee of a lot of laughs.

Laughing is fine, but it can also put a strain on a singer's throat, and there were signs during this Australian tour that Tom's voice was suffering.

It was nothing tragic, just a certain soreness, perhaps from overdoing it in the past year. But when you are a multimillion-dollar property and that income comes from the area of the throat, any sign of trouble has to be taken seriously. Most of us can make do with a cough drop and forget it, but Tom was taken to see specialists who prodded and probed and issued the edict that his tonsils would have to come out—and anyway how come he'd been singing so long without having cracked up?

The newspapers latched on to the "human drama" of the situation. "Tonsils," they implied, "are unimportant, especially in a child. But in an adult, there can be complications even with such a simple operation. As for a singer . . . well, it could be very dangerous indeed."

They added menacingly: "The operation could change the whole timbre of Tom Jones's voice." Change it? In what way? Soften it up, maybe, and that could make it sound ridiculous, coming from such a muscular six-foot frame. Or maybe make it even deeper and throatier. "Oh, well, the hell with it. Get the operation over and done with. Delay might only make matters worse."

So, on a Tuesday morning, Tom's tonsils were re-

75

moved and placed, rumor has it, in a glass bottle. The operation, punctuated by official bulletins, took place at the expensive London Clinic. The operation took about half an hour and went without a hitch. Tom came out of it completely well; not so happy were the telephone operators at the Clinic, besieged with calls from fans. Some just wanted to wish their Tom well. Others declared that, by hook or crook, they'd get hold of those tonsils.

The only problem left was that Tom was put out of action for a while. He missed out on going to the Academy Awards dinner in Hollywood. He'd been invited by Burt Bacharach whose "What's New, Pussycat" had been nominated for an Oscar. And there was an important Variety Club of Great Britain luncheon, with the Duke of Edinburgh as guest of honor.

But Tom, for a change, rested up and gave his throat a chance to recover. And surely he owed it that at least, having given it a terrible beating for the best part of ten years.

Tom simply had been born to sing. Even at home, after the night's show was over, he'd sing along with his records. When he appeared at a club, probably you'd find him, backstage, singing along with the supporting groups. He didn't plan it. It just happened. His throat had had to take it.

Tom also had been smoking up to sixty cigarettes a day. The specialists told him smoking that many cigarettes was ruinous of his throat and general health. Thereafter, when the craving got too great, Tom tried a cigar, but he was warned that cigarettes were out, perhaps forever. Then there was a bruise on his vocal cords, caused, as was to be expected, by the operation, and there also were signs of severe strain on the muscles that produced the voice that produced the excitement.

It is different for opera singers. Mostly, they train from an early age and are taught to breathe properly and relax their throats. They are also taught to overcome their nerves. Tom, in contrast, sang from the soul; he simply got caught up in the mood of his audience and the meaning of the lyrics. He knew, roughly and with the untrained singer's intuition, where he was going wrong, causing strain, but he did not have the discipline that would have enabled him to ease up on those occasions when it was not absolutely important to holler at full blast.

So it was a period of necessary quiet, in many different ways. Tom was also warned to lay off hard liquor, which was difficult because he was an enthusiastic rum and Coke drinker. But at least he was wealthy enough now to obey doctor's orders to the limit: cigars and champagne it would be from now on in. Hang the expense. "I mean, the doctors did say I'd be better off with the long Havana and the vintage champagne."

Problems tend to bring further problems. Maybe it was inevitable that Tom should be involved in a car crash in London in midsummer of this up-and-down year of 1966. He was driving some friends home in his brand-new, bright-red Jaguar when the car skidded and crashed into some railings. The result of this early-hours mishap was a line of stitches over the left eye and a few more marks on the already lived-in face of Tom Jones, pop singer.

At least, "Once There Was a Time" was on the

charts. And it was a double-sided hit, too: "Not Responsible" also was getting a lot of play on radio. This success was encouraging to Tom and Gordon because there was a lot of talk in the industry that Tom had maybe lost the formula for hit records.

When asked about the importance of single hits, Tom always said that the original string of hits in 1965 had established him as a name and that he felt that, as a result, he was accepted more as a performer than just a recording artist. Still, when "Stop Breaking My Heart" stopped selling almost before it had started, he confided to friends that he was worried: "Not because I think my own little world is coming to an end, but just because something must be wrong if people don't bother to buy a record. The fault could simply lie in the material and Lord knows it's hard enough to find the right song at the right time."

This problem has always affected solo singers more than beat groups, many of whom write their own material. Tom was a performer. He wasn't particularly interested in writing his own songs, and, anyway, he figured that there just weren't enough hours in a day to take on extra outlets for his energetic constitution. If a singer builds a name for himself, the best material usually comes to him; he doesn't have to meander around music publishers in search of a good, exclusive number.

Actually, being able to cope with the occasional failure is not something that comes easily to most pop stars. Either they deny that there *is* any fragment of failure, or they blame everybody else in sight, from management to musicians.

A Period of Retrenchment

After only fifteen months in the spotlight, Tom found that even a slight case of "slipped disc" led to an outbreak of the petty bickering that some people indulge in when there is nothing much happening. Rolling Stone Mick Jagger listened to the Jones voice on "Once There Was a Time" and decided it wasn't much of a performance. Tom read the criticism but just wouldn't get himself into a public debate. For one thing, he had earned considerable status as an artist and certainly "didn't need the publicity" stirred up by a public slinging match. And he genuinely thought it was petty for fellow artists to get newspaper space by expressing adverse opinions about each other.

As Tom said: "People can run me down as much as they like. As long as I feel I'm doing the best I can, then I'm happy. But this can be a real funny business. People will run you down behind your back and then treat you like an old mate next time you meet them. I don't get involved. I hope I can always manage to keep out of the arguments. And anyway, some of them are just stunts dreamed up by the newspapers to produce a good story."

It is interesting to note that, even in 1966, Tom was anxious to get into the film business. He was reading scripts and talking them over with Gordon Mills, but he was determined not to make a film just for the sake of making a film. He nursed a private ambition to play a cowboy role but agreed that that ambition was a bit far fetched in view of his still-broad Welsh accent.

That he didn't, in 1966, make a start in films was the result of management advice. There had been more tragedies than triumphs among pop stars who had been enticed into movies, shoved into a poor production with a feeble story and with signposted outbursts of song just to pull in the cash customers. As of this writing, in fact, Tom still hasn't made a film. He must have read hundreds of scripts and synopses, but the fact is that he rapidly became a superstar, and superstars don't have to make do with second-best offers.

For eight long months in 1966 Tom didn't figure in the charts, but his popularity and acceptance were beyond doubt. In the *Melody Maker* poll, announced in September, 1966, he emerged as top British male singer and even got a number six rating in the world section of the same poll. And this achievement was especially significant because the fiery wild man of soul singing had become the first to topple the nice guy with the boy-next-door appeal, Cliff Richard.

The styles and personalities of Cliff and Tom were completely different. Back in 1958–59 Cliff was very much on an Elvis Presley kick, with hips grinding and throw-it-at-'em pelvic thrusts, but then a television producer, Jack Good, had changed his style. Cliff dropped his guitar, toned down his movements, and had a million-seller in "Living Doll," which was nice pop, nothing sinister. From that moment the India-born Cliff, real name Harry Webb, had dominated the male side of pop music in Britain. Unlike Tom, though, he never had much impact in the United States.

In a sense the *Melody Maker* poll heralded the end of an era, a long era that had seen the development of British rockers and was, some four years after Cliff's breakthrough, to see the Beatles emerge and shake up the whole popular music business all over again.

While Tom Jones was selling hard, undiluted sex, being photographed sipping his champagne and tugging on a long cigar, often leering, Cliff was gradually veering over to an active role in religion. He collaborated with evangelist Billy Graham, worked hard in youth fellowship organizations, and was not afraid to speak out on how God and the church had patterned his life—even though he was also a leader in the usually free-and-easy, anything-goes world of pop music. Cliff also had made some good films, such as *Expresso Bongo* and *The Young Ones*, which had widened his appeal and lengthened his unbroken stay at the top.

In any case, Tom the Tiger took over from Cliff the Cleric. And it was undeniable that a change was good for the recording industry.

Cliff was magnanimous in defeat. Said Tom: "Phew, that's a real relief. In these polls, you usually get the youngsters voting and I hoped that my sort of family-entertainer reputation wouldn't put them off me. I know Cliff to be a very nice guy, but personally I prefer singers who put a whole load of guts into their songs."

In a *Melody Maker* "think-in" interview, Tom harked back to the days when he admitted he was a Teddy boy —on the face of it a potential troublemaker, even if these Edwardian-dressed lads often were misjudged. He said: "Yes, I was a Teddy boy. But to most people, Teddy boys just meant gangs. I still like velvet collars, big shoulders and long hair. I got involved in violence, yeah."

81

Tom had belonged to a gang called the Pontypridd Boys, and when they visited a neighboring town, everybody knew who they were. Gang rivalry led inevitably to fights. But he stressed that the Pontypridd Boys never used knives, never actually carried any weapon, even if the boot used to be put in now and again.

"We felt we had to prove ourselves. At that time, older people were more down on teenagers. Today, they are more accepted. I'd walk along down the street past the local club and they would come out and say: 'Look at that animal.' You had to fight to prove yourself. This was all when I was fifteen or sixteen. I got married, of course, and I had to cool it. I got picked on because I was a Teddy boy and then I got picked on because I was a young married man. So I had to prove myself all over again. When I go back home now, the older people say: 'What a lovely boy.' "

In the same interview Tom also gave his views on religion: "Well, when I was young I used to go to the chapel, like most Welsh lads do. And I enjoyed singing hymns. But church I'm not too keen on, because it's not such a nice atmosphere. Sunday School was happy and Gospel singing in New York knocked me out. I believe in God but I don't believe in different types of religions. I pray when I need to, but I never go to church."

As this interview shows, Tom, voted number one singer in Britain in 1966, was more and more involved in the business of giving opinions on things other than singing. It's long been a fact that we expect our pop stars and sportsmen to give views on everything from religion to politics, and we either hang onto their every word or we wrongly blame them for "shouting off about things which they just don't know about."

It was obvious that Tom was coping well. And his popularity was confirmed in the *New Musical Express* poll taken just before Christmas, 1966. True, Tom came second in the British male singer section, but he was voted fifth in the world section, beating such international names as Roy Orbison and Bob Dylan, Tony Bennett, and Frank Sinatra. Tom's television series, started not long before, was taking him into twenty million homes; he had got through to all sections of the community. Shrewd management had given him enough exposure, but not too much.

However, there was one word of warning. Pop polls often tend to reflect what is in the charts at the time of voting. Pop is such a transitory business that fans often can't stretch their minds back to what was going on six months earlier.

And what was going for Tom Jones at the end of 1966 was a song called "Green, Green Grass of Home," which hit the number one spot in three weeks flat and was easily his biggest success since "It's Not Unusual."

Said Tom: "It was the right song. Some numbers are so personal that they can hardly fail. Immediately there is a bond between the singer and the lyrics and the audience. What makes me specially pleased is that it was chosen by me alone. I'd heard it on a Jerry Lee Lewis album called 'Country Songs for City Folk,' and I knew instinctively it was right for me."

Thus a further link was cemented between Tom and the controversial Jerry Lee. The American with the long fair hair and the gimmick of combing it ostentatiously while hammering away at his piano was, as we've seen, a long-time idol of Tom. Certainly Tom has said that Jerry Lee and Gordon Mills were the biggest influences of all on his career. Having recorded the song, Tom made sure that Jerry Lee heard it—he called on the American in his dressing room while Jerry Lee was playing a northern England date and duly received the seal of approval from the long-established American.

"Green, Green Grass of Home" was a story-line song, by no means a typical Jones rocker-raver, but it was instantly recognizable as bearing Tom's trademark. For many fans "Green Grass" remains Tom's most memorable single performance, a good note on which to end Tom's first full year as an international star. His tonsils had gone, but clearly his voice remained at full power.

But not everybody was satisfied. A young university graduate named Jonathan King, who had built a reputation for being extremely outspoken about pop music and had arrived on the strength of a self-penned song called "Everyone's Gone to the Moon," had gone on to become a producer, manager, publicist, promoter, and pundit. Sometimes he made good sense as he waged a battle against the paucity of ideas in the recording industry. But sometimes he seemed way off beam in terms of judgment. Of Tom Jones he wrote, "I don't want to sound anti-Jones but what has he got to offer? He is full of enthusiasm and has a certain animal charm. But he can never be called an entertainer. His television personality comes as near zero as possible.

A Period of Retrenchment

"He moves like an itchy survivor from the early 1950's and sings—nay, shrieks and screams—like a beast from the jungle. There is always a grating edge to his voice. At his quietest he produces a harsh subdued bellow from the lungs, rather than a gentle caress from the throat. No finesse, no subtlety. I don't want to knock Tom—what he is capable of doing, he does well. I do want to criticise the people who claim he is better than he is. An adequate pop star, yes—an entertainer, no."

Yet King was writing about the "adequate" artist who was to become the highest-paid entertainer in the history of British show business. Maybe his style was not to everybody's liking, though his television series and the success of his records seemed to indicate that he was getting through to a good cross-section of the people, but his star status certainly couldn't be denied. True, he was hitting audiences not with a caress or finesse; he was knocking them cold with the power of a sledgehammer. And it's not easy to win an argument with a sledgehammer.

Above: Relaxing in Majorca after appearing on Spanish television and in the famous Tagomago nightclub in Palma.

Left: Toweling-down between shows.

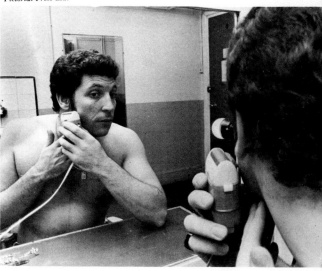

Above: It *is* unusual to find power points in dressing rooms.

Above: Tom with Jill Bennett and Maggie Smith: winners of 1968 Variety Club of Great Britain Awards. Tom was Show Business Personality of the Year.

Below: Tom and two of his four cars.

Tom's $150,000 home in Weybridge, Surrey, 1969.

At home Tom collects guns and swords.

There's always a Jerry Lee Lewis record on the turntable.

Popperfoto

Left: Tom pictured outside the High Court, London, with manager Gordon Mills while Tom was being sued by his first manager, January, 1969.

Left: Tom prepares for his Independent Television series—the most expensive ever made in Britain.

Rex Features Ltd. Photo by Jon Lyons

Above: Tom with one of the guests on his show: Peter Sellers.

Below: Tom relaxes after a show with producer Jon Scoffield and Mary Hopkin.

Above: Manager Gordon Mills (center) with Tom and Engelbert Humperdinck, outside ATV studios in London.

Below: Tom is greeted by Sherri Schruhl, the Flamingo Hotel's official greeter, during his sensational season in Las Vegas.

8 Tom and Engelbert

There is a dreadful amount of phoniness about the recording industry. But in contrast to other areas of entertainment it is not easy to pick out the phony because the finished product is just a piece of shellac and the *sound*—only the sound—matters.

All the same, the pop business is packed with stories of how so-and-so was barely capable of stringing two notes together in the studio, yet ended up with a hit record that earned thousands of dollars. Or of guitarists who had such a limited technique they got past even the three-chord trick only by trial and error, but who were faked up by studio technicians to emerge on disc as virtuoso performers.

Then there were the groups, some of whom simply admitted that they didn't actually play on their records at all. Session musicians were called in and paid comparatively low fees to make the right sounds and then forget it, while the group went out and fooled the fans into parting with hard cash for substandard performances. After all, who actually went to a pop concert to *hear* the artists? It's what could be seen that counted— that and the tension relief from having a good scream or an emotional spasm of tears.

As the sixties passed, the emphasis was placed less on pretty-boy groups and more squarely on those who could actually play imaginative music. But the phoniness was still there in other ways. We knew that certain groups could only record in the early hours of the morning. Or that they had to be high, on drugs or booze, before they could even make a start. Some groups, the Beatles among them, took weeks and weeks working on just one number.

There is never anything phony about Tom Jones. Whatever vocal sound he gets in the studio, he can reproduce faithfully and accurately on stage. Far from giving short measure when he goes on tour, he hands out extra value for the fans who buy his records and want to see just what he can do as a performer.

Tom happens to like recording in the evenings, preferably between seven and ten, simply because he's usually worked late in a cabaret the night before. He goes in prepared to start right away because he's done his homework well in advance.

For the average pop singer, just walking into one of the big studios takes a lot of courage, whether from inside themselves or from inside a bottle, for they have to face real pros. Session musicians are experienced, usually with a lifetime of playing, straight off, just what is placed in front of them. They sight-read music, can switch to any style of music without a flicker of conscious effort. Though comparatively well paid for their long hours, they figure, almost to a man, that pop stars of puny talent are grossly overpaid for being virtually nonmusicians, almost anti-musicians.

Tom Jones had no trouble with the sessions men. He positively bubbled with warmth toward the musicians, greeting them as friends and most definitely as equals. There was no mistaking his confidence in the studio—and he was never reluctant to ask for advice if something seemed to be going wrong.

Tom worked closely with Gordon Mills and with his recording manager, Peter Sullivan. And hang the expense if they wanted a really full-blooded sound! Pay for sixty musicians and the backing singers at the standard session fees is a lot of money. There was precious little change from $2,500.

Professionalism shows itself in many different ways. Tom regarded recording as being just an extension of his live-performance self. He just went in and sang. Even in the early evening when by tradition the pop music world was just waking up, Tom could push out that compelling sense of rhythm. He even took hackneyed lyrics—for example, his version of "Ghost Riders in the Sky," a much-plugged record even when Tom was a boy—and invested them with his own kind of interpretation. There were critics who felt he would be strictly limited in the kind of songs he could sing, but one has only to play through his albums to realize that he can tackle virtually

89

anything. Tom knew just what he wanted, and he had the ability to get it right, almost at the first time of asking.

Gordon Mills, then, had done just what he set out to do. He'd created an international name, and he'd also molded a completely professional entertainer from what was originally very raw material.

So it was no big surprise when Gordon began to look round for another artist to promote and manage. The singer Gordon came up with was a pencil-slim young man named Gerry Dorsey, later to become Engelbert Humperdinck. And as Engelbert Humperdinck his record, "Release Me," was to go straight to the top of the charts and trigger off another sensational pop music career.

Once again, it looked a bit like an overnight-success story. But again it actually represented a long haul to find the right song at the right time for an undoubtedly talented young man. Like ten years! As Gerry Dorsey, Engelbert had his share of fans and praise but got nowhere fast. Born in Madras, India, the ninth of ten children of an engineer, Mervyn, and his wife, Olive, he'd been in England since 1947.

In England, Engelbert studied both piano and saxophone. His mother was a talented singer, and, after a false start in an engineering career, Engelbert had turned to singing. He joined the army, boxed a little, sang a lot, but his experience as a non-com didn't do much for him when he decided to try to make it full time as a singer, in 1956. He was actually making records by 1958, but it was only nine years later that he had any success. His break, as with Tom, came when Gordon Mills decided to manage him.

Like Tom, Engelbert had had a long spell in a hospital with a chest illness—upon the advice of his old friend, Gordon, who made him go to the hospital for a checkup, in which the complaint was discovered. Lack of food was one of the problems; Engel, married, often had to ration himself to pennies a day as his food allowance. Everything changed when Gordon Mills, now supermanager of a superstar, built enough power and prestige to take on an extra client. Three men, all successful, later to build a multimillion-dollar company, were joined together.

Engelbert was launched on an unsuspecting pop world, replete with his new name, by a record release and by an appearance in one of those interminable song contests; this one was at Knokke-le-Zoute, a millionaire playground in Belgium. Most of the reporters there were puzzled by the quiet man with the loud name. The English team won, but that is very much by the way in this kind of nonevent. What was important was the discovery of a fine new talent.

At first sight it seemed tantamount to suicide for Gordon Mills to take on another male singer and expect to build him in the same big-name mold as Tom Jones. A girl singer, yes. A group, okay. Even a symphony orchestra or a troupe of babbling baboons. But the chances of getting two international male stars within a year or so were surely astronomically stacked against him. And the chances of keeping both artists happy were even more dubious.

The pundits prophesied that if Gordon paid too much attention to Engelbert, once "Release Me" had sold its first million copies, then Tom would feel unsettled. And vice versa. In fact, Tom and Engel instantly became great friends and their careers were planned, coolly and deliberately, so that there would be a minimum of clashing interests over the spacing of record releases.

Maybe the most important fact is that the two stars are completely different in terms of performance appeal. While Tom spirals and swivels and spins and jerks, Engelbert works on the cool approach. While singing ballads, Engelbert holds the microphone gently, letting out the words on a wave of sound that, if it could be touched, would feel like velvet.

In the event, both made hit records; both conquered the nightclub world; both earned the screams of teenagers and the respect of adults. But only in the broadest sense did their pop interests clash. And Gordon Mills proved again that he was wise to give up singing and blowing on that harmonica. He had a distinct knack in the tough world of percentages and profits, and if he missed being out there in the spotlight, he certainly didn't let it show.

Meanwhile, Tom Jones made further progress in the charts with "Detroit City," which also came from a Jerry Lee Lewis album. It was the time of Monkee-mania, of songs such as "I'm a Believer" and other teeny-bopper songs. Compared with the weight of a Tom Jones's performance, the competition was light-weight.

Though by now even the knockers were convinced

that Tom's position in show business was assured, there were fears that the teeny-bopper craze would have serious consequences. What teeny-bopper music added up to was simple, purely commercial music played by characters who were strong on personality but mostly light on talent in a musical sense. The effect was terribly contrived.

The Monkees had been created to a formula. A business concern placed an advertisement in a U.S. show-business magazine inviting "crazy-type" boys to attend an audition. The idea was planned every inch of the way. What was wanted was a group of four boys who would be featured regularly on television—a zany kind of pop group who were basically more actors than singers or musicians. The four who got the job were Peter Tork, a banjo-picking folk fan who had languished at near-poverty level around the haunts of Greenwich Village; Micky Dolenz, who had been a child actor and was happily working as a car mechanic; Davy Jones, a successful musical-comedy artist from London who was only vaguely connected with pop music; and Mike Nesmith, a musician at heart who hadn't found how to make real money out of his interest.

The Monkees came through in 1967 and virtually took over the music papers on both sides of the Atlantic. In a way, it was all a mistake that they emerged as record sellers. They had a record out—really as a trailer for the television comedy series—and astonishingly it hit the charts. Suddenly the four lads had to learn how to make their own pop sounds in the studios.

Monkee-mania didn't last long. But for just a while

the spotlight was off the world traveling Tom Jones as the papers rushed to build circulation among the twelve-, thirteen-, and fourteen-year-olds. By comparison, Tom Jones seemed even more a man of the world, with the accent on *man*. There was antiseptic sex from the Monkees and their myriad copyists; there was an air of near rape about the way Tom used his physical assets.

But if some experts felt that pop was going backward again, Tom told the world that he was just not afraid of the future anymore. He told Alan Smith, of *New Musical Express*: "I just don't fear things anymore. I take life as it happens and I trust the people around me. But I've also come to face up to the fact that I'm not so much the guy with a teenage image anymore. I still like to do a few ravers, but the biggest number of my fans are in their mid-twenties and thirties. Nightclubs have now become my main scene, even though I still get a kick out of doing my old act, with the red shirt and the rabbit's foot."

In the same interview, Tom explained how he was getting that deep emotional feeling into his songs. "I act out the songs. I doubt if I could record a song that somebody had given me just the day before. I need to read the words over and over again, to soak them up, to try and squeeze every ounce of meaning out of every word. So many performers just sing a song without really thinking about the deeper meaning.

"On one record, you'll hear me sob with emotion at one part. That just happened. I was so wrapped up with the intensity of the words it just . . . well, sort of happened. Two songs that get me going are 'My Yiddish Momma' and 'My Mother's Eyes'."

The transition, then, was fast. Though Tom's records appealed very much to the teenage element, which still bought the majority of the singles produced, his own shows were pulling in mothers and grandmothers, who had at last found something with appeal for them in a pop business that had created a huge generation gap through the Beatles and the Rolling Stones.

Tom wore his tuxedo, and he looked neat, and he removed his tie when he felt like it, and he whirled his coat, and he sold sex. It didn't come cheaply. He starred at the Talk of the Town night spot in London, and few British artists had, at that time, earned that accolade. A month later he was starring at the London Palladium, and it was a sell-out success. By the end of 1967 he was appearing in the same theater before Queen Elizabeth II in the annual Royal Variety Performance. Society women attended, and they registered precisely the same emotions as had come from teenagers when Tom was barnstorming the dance halls and clubs.

Sometimes Tom admitted to being a bit scared when playing in front of celebrity-stacked audiences. As he looked around a nightclub, he often was able to pick out top names of the business who had long been favorites of his. He found it strange, but satisfying, to be performing for them.

Of his feelings at the Royal Variety Performance at the Palladium, Tom admitted, "I was terrified. It was easily my worst attack of nerves. I was so nervous that my mouth dried up. My top lip stuck to my teeth while I was singing."

Even so, being frightened didn't in any way inhibit Tom's approach to his shortened act. He came on to warm applause, looked nervously up at the Royal Box, and got on with his usual hip-wiggling exhibition. Nobody complained. And the vast television audience who watched the show at a later date came to understand a bit more clearly just what this man was all about.

As for working the London Palladium, long known as the greatest variety theater in the world, Tom got to know it well. During his season there, Tom had, for a period, to relinquish the star dressing room to Jack Benny, and he left a note inviting Jack to help himself to any drinks he fancied from Tom's refrigerator. As a thank you, having done his "Sunday Night at the London Palladium" television performance, Jack left a £1 note on the table. It was inscribed: "This proves that I'm not the stingiest man in the world."

As a partial result of his success, Tom bought a bigger and better patch of his own green, green grass of home, in Sunbury-on-Thames. Called Springfield House, it cost more than $60,000, had five bedrooms, four toilets, two bathrooms, and was stocked with exquisite furniture. Tom excused the extravagance by saying that his old garage just wasn't big enough for the Rolls-Royce. It was all a far cry from a Welsh mining town.

It was a champagne world, and Tom was happy enough to let newspapermen look over his new home, of which he was proud, if not conceited. With some other stars, maybe, it would have looked ostentatious to put their worldly possessions on show, but with Tom it was just the enthusiasm of a working class lad who'd made a killing on the horse races. He still talked down-to-earth talk, slightly mocking his status as a sex symbol for millions.

And the popularity polls for 1967 seemed at first sight to give the lie to his theory that he was moving further and further away from the teenage scene. In the *New Musical Express* poll, he won the "British male singer" section comfortably enough, beating Cliff Richard into second place for the first time in this big-selling weekly. In third place was Engelbert Humperdinck, Tom's stable-mate in the Gordon Mills set-up.

As for the "world" section, Elvis Presley must have had a severe fright when he saw the voting. Elvis had won top place—it had almost become his personal right —for thirteen years, but in 1967 Tom Jones was breathing right down his neck. Only a couple of hundred votes separated them.

Tom took second place to Cliff Richard in the annual *Melody Maker* poll, but he still pipped all the other singers to emerge as second to Simon Dee, compere and disc jockey, in the top "television artist" section.

As Tom and Engelbert became more successful, Gordon Mills had to undertake more and more decision making. He didn't seem to mind. He said, "I don't believe, never have, that any man can honestly say he has more than three genuine friends. So I'm obviously very happy to be able to say that in Tom and Engel I

97

have two of the very best. That's why I'd always fight every inch of the way for them."

Tom, meanwhile, fought every inch of the way for his fans. His twenty-four-hours-a-day, change-of-town-every-night schedules were exhausting. Tom was onstage for an hour every show, packing in at least fourteen energetic songs, never letting up the real physical onslaught for even a moment.

Despite his hectic schedule, however, Tom found time to exchange that glorious, beautiful, magnificent, Welsh-mountainous, coal-carved nose of his for a cute-but-still-bumpy Van Johnson-type nose. The result took some of the terror out of his rugged features, and most certainly he photographed better in profile afterward. After all, the original model had been pulverized in many a teenage tumult.

Tom played the whole business very coolly indeed. Though dozens of show business personalities go in for plastic surgery, Tom somehow felt that a nose job didn't convey quite the right sort of image for a lad from the Welsh valleys. He told newspapermen that the new nose was "an accident."

"I had to have an operation for sinus trouble or something," he said. "When I came out, I noticed the nose was shorter. They must have cut something out of it. I must say I like it better than I did the old one. Ugly it was, when you come to think of it. I didn't dislike it, but then I wasn't madly in love with it. It was in the beer before I'd taken a sip."

Later, Tom was to tell Ray Connolly, of the *Evening Standard:* "I don't think I could have done so well if I hadn't had my nose altered. I think now that it doesn't look as offensive as it did. Before, some people might have thought: 'Well I quite like his voice but I don't like his nose.' So you have to eliminate all those things that put people off.

"My nose and my teeth were the only hang-ups I ever had. I would have had my nose altered even if I hadn't made it this big. I never liked it. If pictures were taken from a bad angle, they made it look ugly and from the same angle my teeth were bad, too. They were decaying, so I had them capped. It would have been nice to walk around and meet everyone and say: 'Look, my nose isn't that bad,' but you can't and so I had it straightened.

"Now I hate to look at the old pictures of me. This nose is how it would have been if it hadn't been broken. You have to have these things done so that no-one will be able to say that there's any one thing about you that puts them off. What I was trying to do was to make myself attractive and presentable to the greatest number of people. You can't afford in this business to have one thing which is ugly about you."

Tom also said that he had to watch what he ate because he put on weight very quickly: "I have to keep myself down, because I can look fat as a pig on camera."

Anyway, in Britain nobody complained—about his face or his performance. No one complained about his hip-swiveling act, even his Royal Variety Performance. Which must have set Tom thinking back to his tour in Australia. As was widely reported at the time: "Police threatened to close a show in Sydney after seeing a performance by British singer Tom Jones." Tom later told the *Daily Mail*: "It was only because I took my shirt off. Why did I take it off? Because it was too hot."

In Brisbane, Australia, on the same tour, a policeman walked into Tom's dressing room, poked him in the chest, and said, "Now listen, you. This is a clean town and it's gonna stay clean. Any trouble from you and we'll shove you inside. Okay?"

Tom said later, "I felt like butting him with me nut, but me hair had just been combed ready for the act." Tom never was too keen on overly officious cops.

Tom's stage performances inevitably led to comparisons with Elvis Presley. And Tom was not unappreciative. As he said during one of his tours, and before Elvis's recent Las Vegas appearance: "It's nice for people to mention Elvis and me in the same breath, but I don't think there is any comparison. He is still a teenage idol. He doesn't go out, nowadays, to prove himself, but I just have to do that.

"I don't think I could ever lead the life of Elvis Presley. He doesn't get out and meet people, and he seems to just shut himself away from the public. I can't argue with the success of his records, but for me having hits would not be enough—not on their own. I just have to get out there and prove myself to a living audience, otherwise I'd go mad."

Actually if Tom was lacking anything during that speeding year of 1967, it was simply that the right film opportunity hadn't come along. He could, obviously, have followed Elvis Presley and churned out similar

100

productions based on similar stories, and let the films play to Jones-starved millions all over the world. Sixty prints of one movie would reach a bigger audience in one evening than Tom could play to in a month or more, but he knew that Presley movies were lightweight and that the public was cooling off. No longer did it think that any Presley was better than no Presley at all.

It's hard to think of Tom as a frustrated person. But he did feel that a really important movie would put the seal on his arrival as a complete entertainer. There was a limit to what he could do in any one country—after all, he had his regular hit records and his big shows and top-rated nightclub performances. What else was there? Only a film.

But, movie or no, there was to be no letting up in the drive to build more bricks on the foundations of Tom's career. According to Gordon Mills: "Tom hasn't really reached his peak. The first time I saw him I knew that he would be the biggest. I still get frustrated even now because his enormous talent still has not been fully recognised. I've seen most of the world's top acts but Tom never fails to amaze me. Each performance is as if it's his last. But he quite definitely is the highest-paid entertainer in Britain."

With all the success Tom's personality didn't change. It could have all gone to Tom's head, but it didn't. He still spent hour after hour autographing pictures for the fan clubs, and whenever he could, he'd invite fans backstage for a chat. "He hasn't become at all big time," said one old friend.

101

One of the Squires said of him: "He has helped all of us around him, all the time, mostly with his sense of humour. One of his favorite escapades when he was happy was to go racing down the street, slapping his backside like he was riding a horse.

"No, this guy is just the same as he ever was. Even if he does now smoke cigars and drive a Rolls-Royce. You could never say he'd become big-headed. He'll be up there with Tony Bennett and Frank Sinatra, that's for sure. Though he still likes to do the earthy blues stuff, he's also beginning to like standards."

Prophetic words, as it happened, even if few would have thought it possible at the time.

9 Tom and Elvis and Las Vegas

Tom Jones spent Christmas, 1967, with his wife and son, his mother and father (who had moved into his old home at Shepperton), and his collection of records. For a change, he gave his voice a rest. And he didn't look like a man with a problem as he did a great demolition job on a crate of champagne. But the problem was there all the same.

As he surveyed the bookings already made for him in the next twelve months, Tom knew they were worth a million dollars—plus. "I'm Coming Home" was soaring high in the world charts. He had engagements in Las Vegas and New York, important concert appearances—while his recent tour in Britain with the Ted Heath big band showed that, to a great extent, he had moved out of the teenage-screamer bracket.

His problem simply was: Which way do I go now? Uppermost in his mind remained the question of breaking into films. He said: "There is one story we like. It would have me as a sort of playboy, racing hydroplanes all round the West Indian beaches and it's an action role, which would suit me. Really, there is not much singing, maybe just one number over the credits, but the most important thing is that it's all action." Unfortunately that film idea came to nothing, like all the others before.

He also thought about his fans, about how they tended to fall into an older age bracket, how he would face the challenge of being a British artist playing the top nightclub dates in Las Vegas, where stars such as Sammy Davis, Jr., Dean Martin, Tony Bennett, and, at that time, Judy Garland were regulars. He said, "I have to realise that the people coming to see me nowadays are from my own age upwards, not from my age downwards. They see me as a singer who gives them what they want in the way of songs and who is sincere in what he sings. I am sure they know that when I sing something I mean it. I always said that when I got to Las Vegas, I'd go in big. If I want to last in this business, I have to go for the best, not crawl in by the back door and start working up. . . ."

Going in big meant earning big money, say, $1 million for thirteen weeks' work—even enough money to indulge Tom's loyal habit of phoning home to wife and son every day, often talking for half an hour at a time.

Moreover, the Vegas date showed that the transition was going well. In every sense, it was an object lesson in shrewd management. The usual train of events was disastrous for 50 percent, at least, of all successful record makers: a hit record, immediate promotion, loss of public interest because of an inability to put on a good eye-catching show, a slump in record sales—and near oblivion. But Tom had hit the top with records, and that had involved only a fraction of his talent. With his Vegas date he had moved into the nightclub circuit with the established names, and his achievements made the Jones career unique.

Ironically, there were people who felt Tom should get back into the pure rock and roll field. Every so often, in pop music, when there is a lull in the treadmill of new talent, the pundits take a long look backward. In Tom's case, the lull came in 1968. Nothing much happened in terms of new sensations, so, they thought, let's try to revive old-style rock and roll. Let's rejuvenate the oldies—Little Richard and Gene Vincent and Jerry Lee Lewis. Let's get some of that old-time excitement into pop music again. Let's belt out some foot-stomping dance rhythms. And if Little Richard and the other oldies are just a shade too old for teen-age tastes, well, there's also that ex-rocker, Tom Jones, who is as skilled in the rocker industry as any of 'em.

But Tom and Gordon Mills were much too skilled to be drawn. Tom was almost 28, and there were dangers in looking backward. He'd seen Jerry Lee Lewis playing *Othello*, no less, in a rock and roll version of the Shakespearian play on Broadway, but the idea of trying something similar never entered the discussion. As Tom said: "Rock and roll music is for the younger people. Sure, it dominated my life when I was a kid. But you don't gain anything by looking backwards, so if there is a rock and roll revival, you won't find me a part of it."

In fact, there was no revival. The drape jackets were dusted off and dry-cleaned, and the drainpipe trousers were pressed, but pure rock, in the old style, was part of history. Tom was beyond that—and loving every moment of it.

Still, even if his career did mean really leaving the past to look after itself, Tom still relished the idea of occasionally doing a raving, berserk-type single, just as a change from the big beaty ballads that had boosted him into the Top Twenties of the world.

Thus, when, early in 1968, he won the *Disc* magazine popularity poll, Tom said to journalist Penny Valentine: "Going berserk is a great thing, but you have to find the right song."

Tom also talked to Penny Valentine about his personal philosophy: "Show business is an easy business to make friends in. Of course there are some people whom you give an inch to and they take a mile, and there are any number of annoying people who only want to talk about the business all the time. But I honestly believe that my life now belongs to the public.

"Fans often drop round to the house and have a cup of tea. They are very nice. And people who grumble about their private life being their own business just annoy me. After all, you can always build a wall around your house so that nobody can get near you—if you're really all that worried."

Tom also admitted that sometimes the sheer exhaustion of constant traveling got him down, saying: "If

I've got to travel somewhere, then I'll do it. The place I'm in is unimportant. Half the time I don't know where I am. It's just a stage and an audience that counts. I don't even like taking a holiday. My wife used to say to me: 'Now how about going to so-and-so this year,' and I just used to mutter: 'Look, don't bother me about things like that.' "

Then he added: "I decided quite a while ago that the best policy in life is to make the best of everything. You meet so many people who moan about everything, they want to do this and that, and they're never satisfied and they're never happy."

Tom's statements about privacy and the public were particularly appropriate because by mid-1968 practically the whole world knew Tom Jones's face and recognized it instantly. This in itself brought its own problems. To many people there was something suspect about anybody who actually made a living out of being a professional pop singer. The groups, long-haired and scruffy most of them, were suspect because they looked effeminate, yet had an extraordinary effect on teenage girls. To the rowdies, the groups were regarded as "easy meat." Most groups had stories to tell of being ambushed by young punks, insulted, and sometimes roughed up.

Tom was different. Tom was a pop singer, but he fitted into the Hollywood leading-man category. The shoulders were broad and the hips slender. He looked as if he could take care of himself in a fight, but there was no shortage of half-drunk blusterers who wanted to put him to the test.

One evening, as Tom sat with a handful of journalists in the Trader Vic bar of the Hilton Hotel in London, his essentially realistic viewpoint came through. "There they are," he said, "these characters who are spoiling for a fight. They come up, leering, in a club or bar somewhere and the drink does the talking for them. They have that insolent look about them. You can pick 'em out a mile away. They say, trying to look you in the eye, that you couldn't punch your way out of a paper bag.

"And I can feel the muscles twitch. It is one of the toughest things in this business, this having to keep out of trouble when someone is just about begging for a punch on the nose.

"What I'd like to do is beat 'em clean across the room, but I have to think how it'd look in the newspapers. *Pop Star in Brawl,* and the people who don't know how it started off say, 'Oh, those singers. They're just hooligans. Straight out of the gutter.' So you play it cool."

It was easy to ridicule some of the long-haired group members. And it was simplicity itself for them to be barred, purely because of the way they looked, from hotels and bars. But Tom was smartly tailored and immaculately manicured: he looked what he was—a millionaire of song, perfectly at ease in luxurious surroundings. In fact, what really annoyed some of the other customers was his essential toughness. Watching the waitresses and the matrons going genuinely ga-ga as he posed for pictures—you didn't have to be a woman to realize what basic animal magnetism was all about.

Maybe a man escorting a girl who went glassy-eyed

just at a glimpse of Tom Jones could be excused for feeling like challenging Tom, to prove his own masculinity. What couldn't be excused was the male equivalent of bitchiness, the suggestion that Tom was somehow a servant of the public, even when relaxing offstage, and was there to be insulted or mocked if the opportunity came along.

Some actors have said how they got inveigled into public punch-ups by creepy characters who want to prove they can thump a man who has launched a thousand thumps in movies. Guys such as Robert Mitchum were not so patient. But what was okay for a self-confessed hell-raising film actor was by no means right for a pop singer.

Tom was exposed to many challenges as he set about conquering the last bastions of the U.S. nightclub belt. At every engagement he was given police protection as he went into the clubs and cabaret rooms. His safety was guaranteed by presidential-type security arrangements—no point in taking chances. After all, there could just be a nut lurking around, ready to take a poke at the face that occasioned so many sighs. But for the most part the police were there to hold off the women.

Tom's big starring date at the Flamingo Hotel in Las Vegas was sensational, even by the ballyhoo standards of U.S. show business. Elvis Presley and his wife drove more than four hundred miles to see for themselves what this new international star was all about. The audience, who had paid dearly for the privilege, stood and cheered, and there was Elvis Presley himself, standing and cheering. Afterward Elvis said, "He's fantastic. There has never been anyone to touch him, not here. He is great."

What the star-studded audiences didn't know was that there were nights when Tom had problems with his voice. He was making the notes all right, those high flying sounds, but it was a struggle. Doctors diagnosed that Tom was suffering because of the lack of moisture in the Nevada air. So he was advised to stay in his room all day, get as much sleep as possible, and get up only at night when the outside atmosphere cooled down.

Tom, then, became even more of a night person. With most of each day lost in sleep, he was happy enough. He never did like losing out on his slumber.

Tom's second meeting with Elvis Presley was regarded as a pop summit conference. Chris Hutchins, Tom's press representative, recalled the scene for *Disc* magazine. At exactly midnight the doors of the main lounge swung open and—surrounded by his wife, bodyguard, Joe Esposito, and eight Memphis boys—in marched Elvis, clad in Carnaby Street suit and long cigar, and made for a ringside table.

"As Tom began his act, Elvis was transfixed. His early life must have come flooding back as he watched the Jones boy twitching his hips and moving around the stage like never before. Elvis began beating the table in time to the music, jumping up and down in his seat and eventually standing up to lead the standing ovation which has become the order of the day for Tom at the Flamingo."

110

Tom and Elvis and Las Vegas

After it was all over, the two stars got together. Elvis told Tom that he was "sensational." And then he told how he had only appeared at Las Vegas once, at the Frontier Hotel some eleven years before, and had died the death. As Elvis said: "I don't think anyone knew what I was all about when I stepped on stage and started those hip movements ... wow, man, they just went right off me."

Elvis definitely was not handing out the usual mutual-admiration show business rigamarole when he recalled memories of Tom's career so far. "I was in the coach with the boys a few years back and 'Green, Green Grass' came on the radio. We were feeling homesick for Memphis anyway and when we heard this we just broke up and cried. One of the boys phoned the radio station and requested it again and the disc jockey played it four more times in succession. And we just sat in the bus crying."

At the end of this informal chat, as Elvis and his entourage moved off, Tom signed some pictures as a reminder of a top-level pop powwow. Then Tom, relaxing into the early hours of the morning, pondered on the time, not so long before, when Elvis was one of his hero figures, a great untouchable so remote from ordinary mortals that the very idea of a tête-à-tête was out of sight.

Meanwhile, in Britain, "Delilah" was the latest Tom Jones hit, and the lyrics came under fire by some people, including a couple of influential disc jockeys. In fairness, Delilah was basically a song of violence. It told of a man who found his girl being unfaithful and killed

111

her—an act of revenge on the spur of the moment. It was a meaningful song with a point to make.

Tom by now was used to the old trick of being dragged into a controversy and was skilled in giving a factual but unsensational reply. He agreed that it was a tough story. He denied that the song actually glorified killing. He said that the main point, as he saw it, was that the killer was immediately sorry for what he had done and was not unhappy that he was going to be punished for the crime. And he added: "But there's always something to knock, isn't there!"

One could understand how he felt. Pop music was expanding its ideas. The lyrics were actually finding something to say. The days of getting away with trite, banal couplings of moon-and-June and love-and-turtle-dove had largely vanished, and the sigh of relief could be heard all around an industry too long dominated by tatty sentimentality.

Pop itself was developing muscles, and that pleased Tom Jones very much indeed. He found, too, that in the United States the industry was no longer dominated by British groups. That fact alone helped him build his reputation. He was no longer merely just a part of the traffic crossing the Atlantic—he was a brand leader. A few years earlier he'd just have been a fragment of the rock and big beat exodus from Britain. Now he was being introduced, at top level, by stars such as Jack Jones, and it was easier to get rid of the image created by his early records.

As "Help Yourself" followed "Delilah" into the charts, Tom had plenty to look back on, even if his star career had spanned only three years. Among fourteen singles there had been only a few that had not been wild successes; his "market" had grown along with his status; and he'd jetted to Australia, New Zealand, the United States, and all over Europe. As Tom said over and over again, "It's better than working on a building site, isn't it?"

In the summer of 1968 Tom did his first big spectacular television show in London. The reaction was fantastic, especially when he launched into what was surely his most violent performance of "Land of a Thousand Dances." His body seemed inhabited by a thousand demons, all fighting to get out through the sleek tuxedo that stretched over it. The headlines suggested that it was the sexiest vocal exhibition yet on television, but Tom wouldn't be drawn. He said only that it was one of his all-time favorite songs, and that he played it by ear. If it seemed sexy, well, all right, but he was really just himself doing what came naturally.

In fact, while there were still no film plans, there were some tremendous developments in the television field. A first series of television spectaculars in color, with an enormous production budget and an international list of guest names, was announced for sale around the world. The series was a logical development. After all, there was a limit to the number of personal appearances Tom could make, but a television series could be seen by millions of people at the same time.

Elvis Presley had been faced with the same problem, but he had solved it by making two or three full-length feature films a year rather than television shows.

Surprisingly, later in the year more poll results showed that Tom's popularity with the young fans wasn't suffering at all, even though he was slanting himself more directly at a more mature audience. He walked off with the *New Musical Express*'s "top male singer" award, beat Cliff Richard decisively this time. He lost by a handful of votes to Elvis in the "world singer" category, but Elvis had a loyal and highly organized fan club who responded instantly and collectively to an invitation to vote. Tom, though always willing to be helpful to his fans, was not backed by a vast official organization—another example of good thinking. There had been several scandals about get-rich-quick organizers who took money from fans and failed to provide a decent service in return.

There was an upset in the *Melody Maker* poll. Tom was beaten by Scott Walker. It was an ironic result. Scott Walker was American by birth, though he had been working in Britain for several years—first as part of the Walker Brothers' trio and later as a solo act. Tom was essentially the exaggerated extrovert; Scott was the complete introvert, sometimes giving the impression that he hated all things to do with pop music.

Scott, most of the time, was moody and unapproachable, shielding himself from his doubts by retiring into a shell. He complained bitterly about the screams that greeted him onstage, even to the point of issuing edicts that fans should "keep quiet and hear what I'm doing."

It was strange that this reluctant pop star should take over from the phenomenal Tom Jones, but part of the reason could have been that Tom had spent so much time in the United States. In pop music absence from the scene for a few months can bring problems.

Anyway, as this surprise result hit the headlines, Tom's management took space in the *Melody Maker* to announce "A smash in Las Vegas—Elvis said he was the greatest—a sensation at the London Palladium. A phenomenal seller of records—more than thirty million in three years. The most successful entertainer Britain has ever produced. Congratulations."

If Tom had missed out on keeping his popularity poll crown as top British singer, he was able to prove by his achievements that he was ahead of the "opposition." What's more, he went out on a fifteen-town tour of Britain and again they had to dust off the standing-room-only notices. The point was made.

The British tour was vintage Tom. He leaped out on-stage in his blue three-piece suit, the blue bow tie inevitably removed at the end of the first number to allow unrestricted viewing of a throbbing Adam's apple. The Ted Heath orchestra, the Squires, and a string section provided the background as Tom roared into "Turn on Your Love Light," an early tribute to his old hero, Jerry Lee Lewis.

There were screams. In fact, there seemed to be nothing but screams. Tom said how hot it was up there on-stage. "Take your coat off then," yelled the willing women. "And your trousers . . ."

There was nothing startling in that kind of exchange at a pop-show one-nighter. Except that the voices belonged to middle-aged women, often to women sitting next to their husbands. "Keep it clean," instructed

Tom, with a leer that soon changed into a self-mocking smile. If the show had stopped after just that one number, it would probably have been value enough for the fans.

"I Can't Stop Loving You," sang Tom—and, "At least please start, Tom," came from a bespectacled woman who looked as if she'd been through secretarial college at least twenty years before. "Hard to Handle," sang Tom—and there was uproar. Married women old enough to have teenage daughters collapsed in their seats as Tom seared the atmosphere with an almost vicious vocal attack.

The eloquent hips swiveled and swerved. The fingers jerked in ten separate spasms. A leg bent and straightened violently. "Danny Boy," "Delilah," "Help Yourself," "It's Not Unusual," on to the finale: "Land of a Thousand Dances"—a larger-than-life repetition of the number that shook rigid an audience of millions on television.

Tom leaned forward confidentially. "I need a little woman," he said. And several hundred women offered themselves up, unhesitatingly, in a kind of mass sacrificial service.

It was easy to see what it was that made Tom tick: first, though not necessarily foremost, the voice, which had a smoky edge but switched mood from song to song; second, the untamed body, responding to the lyrics and the bite of the brass section, contorting in movements that couldn't have been planned because so much of the act depended on the reaction he was getting from different parts of the audience.

116

Said one front-seat spectator, "He's too loud and he's got a punch-drunk face and he sure isn't a Sinatra." The pinstripe-suited man's wife was with him—flushed, fraught, and almost finished.

Afterward, wide-eyed women gathered in the star's dressing room. "You must be dead tired," said one. "And yet you have another show to do." Tom grinned that slow-burning grin that implied about a hundred different things at once. "I don't *get* tired, love," he said. "Doing a show is like getting a bit of exercise, say going eight rounds in a gymnasium. I'm just not tired, love."

A suggestion of a one-more-time pelvic twitch, and it was obviously too much for the inquiring female. She retreated, taking a glazed look with her. Was his act actually erotic? For a male, it's an almost impossible question to answer. Its effect on women left little doubt.

Tom put as much into rehearsals for this important British tour as he did into the actual shows.

Tom's show was deliberately a riot-raising performance, but that had long been part of the pop music tradition. The difference was that, for the first time, Tom was using his masculinity to stimulate a mass of women older than the usual teenaged one-nighter addicts.

What was equally certain was that Tom, offstage, was showing not a sign of the conceit, the awareness, that one might expect from a man who had power over women. His dressing room, full of casual callers—a disc jockey taping a radio interview, relatives, journalists, mates from Wales—was also full of lighthearted banter, followed by serious moments of conversation as

117

Tom talked over a brass phrase or a string-section sequence with Gordon Mills.

Tom's mother and father sat there, looking helplessly proud of their boy who'd broken away and found world fame. And Tom, as he introduced them to his show business friends, made no attempt to hide the pride he felt for them.

Always, however, there was the fear that this constant strain would lead to Tom's throat's constricting. There was certainly a bad scare when he arrived in Vienna just before Christmas, 1968. He was in the middle of a massive European tour, country by country, building up a following that was already strong as a result of his disc sales. A bad bout of influenza affected his vocal cords, and he had to cancel dates in Berlin, Frankfurt, and Bremen. In one show in Berlin, he cracked vocally, so he cut the performance short and went to bed for a couple of days.

His throat inflamed and painful, Tom was given antibiotics, but what hurt him most was having to cancel performances. In fact, he insisted on staying in Europe at the end of his scheduled tour to fit in some of the dates he had missed.

Meanwhile, his record, "A Minute of Your Time," was making predictable progress up the world charts, though some critics felt that this wide-ranged ballad was one of Tom's weaker discs. Tom, of course, realized that it was impossible to please everybody with every record, but he constantly stressed that he, Gordon Mills, and Peter Sullivan were not prepared to record bad numbers simply because they had a strong commercial

Right: Tom shares a plate with Mary Wilson of the Supremes.

Below: Tom receives congratulations after his opening show in Las Vegas from Dionne Warwick and Michael Caine.

Popperfoto

Popp

Right: Taking no chances, Tom is surrounded by security guards.

Left: Tom's 1969 coming-home present to himself: a Rolls-Royce Silver Phantom, equipped with color TV.

Syndication International and Sunday Mirror

Tom

Fox Photos

Above: Tom meets Queen Elizabeth II after the Royal Variety Performance at the London Palladium, November, 1969.

Below: Tom performs with world champion entertainer Bob Hope.

Camera Press Ltd. Photo by Peter Mitchell

ox Photos

Above: Tom shares a joke with Prince Philip. Herb Alpert stands next to Tom.

Syndication International

Right: Tom smoking one of his cigars, "on doctor's orders."

Tom on stage during a concert tour of Great Britain.

Above: The essential Tom Jones.

Right: A well-deserved break — champagne is also "doctor's orders."

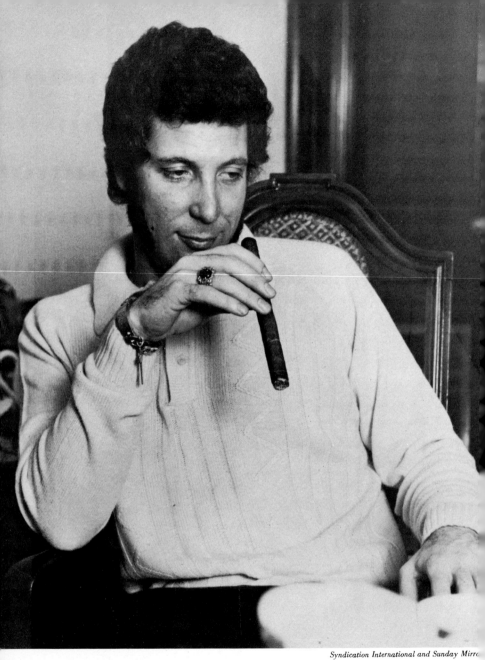

A satisfied and pensive Tom Jones.

chance. "To be honest, I'd rather do a song that might not even make the Top Twenty than churn out some commercial thing that had no artistic merit at all," Tom said.

At the end of his third year in the big time, Tom really felt he knew his way around the pop industry. What he really wanted was more time to spend at home, watching his son grow up and enjoying his family life. But only a part of Tom Jones belonged in that luxury home. The rest had to be spread over all parts of the world where pop was played. And that, he felt, was a fair enough exchange for all that pop music had given him.

10   Taking Stock

By 1969 most people assumed that Tom Jones had fulfilled all his ambitions, that there was nothing left for him to conquer. They saw him as a vocal mountaineer who had no Everest left to climb. But Tom was the sort of character who simply invented new pinnacles when he felt that none existed in fact.

What he wanted to do more than anything was to make his $21.6 million first television series a complete success. He spent almost all his time at the studios at Elstree, making sure that everything went exactly right.

Sir Lew Grade, head of Associated Television, told the press that he was convinced that the Tom Jones television series would make Tom the greatest of all singing stars. Adjectives such as *greatest* are bandied around like so much confetti in the rarefied atmosphere of big-time show business, but the worldwide interest in this series was so immediate and enthusiastic that in this case the rave was justified.

All Tom said was: "One thing I have learned is that one should relax more on television. It is different in a theatre, where you have somehow to reach out and hit the back walls with power. I used to think the same in front of the television cameras—go out and belt away hard, put on a terrific show each time by working at full pitch. Now I feel more relaxed."

If he wasn't talking business, he was talking about his new home at Weybridge, Surrey, and how he was installing a billiards room and a gymnasium and a sauna bath. Tom had always had a weight problem. He'd given up drinking gallons of beer, but he was still prone to putting on extra inches round the waist and hips. Sure, it meant he had more hips to wiggle, but Tom took the whole business of exercise and keeping fit very seriously indeed. "Sweating it out on stage isn't enough," he said. Which is why he wanted a sauna bath.

Tom's value in hard cash was, by 1969, impossible to estimate. Probably Tom himself did not know how much he was worth. He carried around maybe $250 in case of emergency, and if he wanted anything that cost more, he'd order it and have the bill sent to his accountant. He rarely remembered to carry a checkbook.

His one minor complaint was that it was now virtually impossible for him to go back to see his old friends in Wales. He said: "They would understand, my old mates would, but there are so many other people —people I barely knew even when I was living in Pontypridd. They'd make demands, I suppose, like

122

autographs and so on, but I just think it would be uncomfortable."

Still, Tom kept the whole thing in perspective. He felt, quite honestly, that he had the vocal talent to become the best, but he also felt that to be up there in the Sinatra-Bennett-Williams category needed something extra, something that probably came from experience. At the same time, he never for a moment doubted the value of his voice.

Said Chris Slade, one of the Squires, "That confidence was always there. It was almost an arrogance, in that he was never afraid to tell people that he could sing and sing well."

Chris Slade recalled an occasion several years before, in a small club in Cardiff, Wales, when Danny Williams was booked to top a bill. Danny was a tiny black boy from South Africa, a gentle-voiced ballad singer who made his disc name with a beautiful version of "Moon River." His fame didn't last long, almost certainly because it was virtually impossible to find a song as good as that Henry Mancini number, but for a while he was one of the most played disc artists in Britain.

Danny naturally closed his act with "Moon River." But midway through it, a massive Welsh voice soared out, joining in with the star of the show, powering through the final phrases and, if anything, holding onto the final notes even longer than Danny. Heads turned, eyes probed through the darkness to see which local loudmouth had got into the act. And there, near the bar, was the culprit. A head sporting the Tony Curtis hairstyle was thrown back, the Tom Jones voice seeming to get louder and louder. It was a cheeky, insolent gesture. But Tom liked making sure his voice would be heard—so determined was he that he returned to the club for a rerun of the incident the very next evening.

It was the sort of thing Tom had seen in many a Hollywood movie. "Unknown takes over from the star and finds instant fame and fortune." Only it just didn't work out that way for Tom Jones—not at once, anyway.

Years had to be worked through before Tom was sitting in the star dressing room of the television studios at Elstree, Hertfordshire and making that first all-important series meant a lot of hard work. He was waked at seven, driven in a Bentley to the studios by eight, then went straight into a rehearsal of the day's shooting. Then there was a snatched lunch before the afternoon's filming. Most days Tom didn't get home until after nine in the evening.

At the studios were reporters from all over the world, from Turkey, India, Australia, from anywhere where pop records were played. All sought the same basic information. "Just how do you explain your impact on our womenfolk, Mr. Jones?" Tom found it difficult keeping a grin off his face. For the thousandth time he'd explain that he wasn't aware of doing anything particularly different onstage, that he just sang and let his body reflect what the lyrics meant to him. "Thank you for coming along, gentlemen, and I'd just like to say that I would very much like to visit your country one day," he would add.

By May, 1969, Tom was back in America, opening at the Copacabana in New York. In the *New Musical*

Express, Derek Johnson reported: "All hell broke loose in the vicinity of the Copa. The police barricades were up in force, the screamers were out en masse and there was an electricity in the air.

"One veteran reporter remarked: 'I ain't seen nuttin' like it since Sinatra in 1957'. Tom's entire season at the Copa was completely sold out three weeks in advance of the opening. And such was his enormous confidence that he didn't even bother to turn up for final rehearsal—his manager Gordon Mills supervised the band call.

"The show itself was typical Tom, but the reaction was unbelievable. The audience consisted of eighty per cent women and my reporter friend said that all the guys had gone bowling! And those women set up a barrage of screaming, the like of which I have never heard in a night-club. I saw one middle-aged woman offer Tom a Kleenex with which to mop his brow, then gleefully stuff the sweat-soaked tissue into her handbag to treasure for ever.

"They stood on the tables, they jumped and shouted —and in the end the waiters had to form a human chain to get Tom off stage. Prior to this, I had been inclined to think that Tom's international image had been somewhat exaggerated. But make no mistake, everyone in America is talking about him and he really is in the superstar league here."

In hard financial terms, Tom broke the thirty-year-old box-office record at the Copa, which had presented virtually every big name in show business as attractions. And when he passed through other parts of the

United States the box office takings soared to astronomical heights—in Connecticut, San Francisco, Los Angeles. This sort of business had to be reflected in the album charts. Statisticians, to whom facts meant more than performances, were astonished that six out of nine available Tom Jones albums were in the *Billboard* charts at the same time, and four of them had already won him Gold Discs for million-dollar sales.

Tom wasn't blasé about his success. He told reporters just how proud he was to call Elvis Presley a friend. He paid gracious tributes: "Elvis taught me you've just got to be free when you sing, move with the music and not be tense or all keyed up. I'm not kidding myself. I know it's my earthy style—sex, animal magnetism, call it what you like. But first and foremost it's just me."

Bernard Barry, in Las Vegas, reported: "He's become the hottest show-business property in America and that is not forgetting Frank Sinatra or Elvis.

"He's at the Flamingo until July 2, but two other hotels, the gaudy Romanesque Caesar's Palace and the incredible 25-million dollar International Hotel, with the largest showroom in Las Vegas, not to mention a golf-course on the third floor, are both willing to pay plenty to lure Mr. Jones away from his Flamingo hotel suite.

"Their ardor and enthusiasm have been fanned by Jones' phenomenal reviews and capacity crowds. It's more than just capacity—burly armed guards have literally had to throw out fans who have tried to charge into the Flamingo showroom. If they sold seats on the chandeliers, they would fill them. Every show is booked

solid for the entire season and that's pretty unique for
a town that is so blasé about stars, great stars, like Ray
Charles and Ella Fitzgerald. But the hysterical audience was not made up of swooning teenyboppers or little
blondes with freshly-ironed hair. They were mothers in
minks and a battalion of hard-faced business girls who
had motored some 300 miles to Vegas to be at the show.
'If I don't get in, I'll blow the place down,' shouted one
mild-mannered young lady. Security guards didn't
know whether to arrest her or let her in."

And Tom was saying, by way of explanation,
"They're the forgotten generation. I used to perform
to the younger crowds in the ballrooms, which was fine
while I had a hit. But when I wasn't in the charts, the
crowds drifted away. My last show, in a half-filled ballroom, was about two-and-a-half years ago."

Tom rented Paul Newman's Hollywood home for his
eight-week stay in Los Angeles. In desperation, Paul
Newman wrote to Tom: "Please tell everyone you are
renting my Hollywood house, not my Connecticut house
which I'm living in now. There is a constant vigil kept
outside here by ardent Tom Jones fans who certainly
don't want to know me!"

Later, in London, Tom's press agent, Chris Hutchins,
was to relate how Frank Sinatra had stopped the show
at Caesar's Palace, having seen Tom, his parents, and
party arrive for the performance. Frank simply announced: "Ladies and gentlemen, there is a very special
young man in the audience tonight. He is number one in
the world today and I am his number one fan—Mr. Tom
Jones."

The boss of the Flamingo, Alex Shoofey, said, "Tom is the most sensational performer ever to hit Las Vegas." And *Variety* magazine reported: "A thousand people a night see the Jones dynamo issuing his numbing electricity. Most of his fifty minutes is peak decibel level, pulverizing each tune into abject submission."

Tom's return to Britain was greeted as a national event. *Welcome home to a superstar*, screamed the headlines. He landed at London Airport, with a new $35,000 Rolls-Royce Phantom Six limousine waiting for him, along with a gaggle of fans. His home, standing in seven acres of ground, had been redecorated while he was away. He'd been gone six months, achieving his greatest triumphs.

Welcome home, Jones the Conqueror! roared another headline. And the conqueror can issue orders to his minions. At any rate, dozens of top stars rushed to be on Tom's next television series: Raquel Welch, Shelley Berman, Nancy Wilson, Anthony Newley, Sammy Davis, Jr., Little Richard, Bobby Darin, Blood, Sweat and Tears—a varied big-name list representing just about every category of show business.

On the financial side there were other triumphs, reflected in a newly formed public company, Management Agency and Music, which was comprised of Tom, as principal asset, plus Gordon Mills and Engelbert Humperdinck. The company initially offered shares in itself on the London Stock Market at $1.59 a share. Tom, it was reported, owned 863,750 of the shares, worth $1,375,759. In just a month or so, the stock increased in value by $4,235,051, which meant that Tom was a millionaire five times over, at least on paper. And there were other things to take into consideration: current earnings, lump sums held over from the start of his stardom. Nobody would quibble with anyone who estimated his value at $7.2 million.

The first stars to go public were the Beatles, who had their Northern Songs organization. It was easy to see why they did so: income tax, which was often levied at such a crippling rate that high-income stars handed over 95 per cent of their income in taxes—unless special arrangements, such as public companies, were made. It was all explained by a tax expert.

"A big star earns the money fast and has to pay the full rate of income tax, after expenses. But if he forms a public company, the allowable expenses are much greater. He can run cars, employ staff, pay the bills out of the company funds as opposed to taking it straight from his own pocket. Many people made a lot of money by investing in Northern Songs, but that was a safe enough bet. There was little chance that Beatle songs would suddenly lose popularity. But the big problem with marketing an artist's talent is that they can fall from favour and so the share value would inevitably drop."

One might expect the stock market valuation based on his talents to give Tom Jones something to worry about. But he simply carried on working and let his financial advisers do the worrying. His voice held out, his confidence was at boiling point—and they were spending well over $240,000 on each of his television shows, about eight times the usual amount lavished on such musical spectaculars in Britain.

Why was so much money spent on the Tom Jones series? Tom Jones was about the only entertainer who could completely bridge the generation gap, particularly in the United States, where they had teenage shows, with a strictly limited age group appeal, or they had the adult shows, such as the casual, highly polished Andy Williams shows. The Tom Jones spectaculars were aimed at both groups and were planned for the generation-gap slot of 7:00-8:00 P.M. A really big star was needed to get into this neglected "all-family" field, and Tom had shown himself to be the ideal choice.

As Tom worked away at yet another series, the greatest pride in the Jones camp was that of Gordon Mills. Gordon particularly liked to tell people that Tom was the hottest artist in the world. Most people agreed, but Gordon's pride was in the fact that he'd seen it all coming, years back when Tom was lucky to find enough loose change to buy a hot dog.

Certainly 1969 went down as the biggest year of all for the galloping superstar. He won popularity polls. He sold records. He dominated new areas of show business. The years of struggle were really over now. In fact, Tom could have stopped singing altogether and simply lived in luxury on the interest from his investments.

But a life of leisure simply didn't appeal. Tom loved to sing.

130

11   Anatomy of a Superstar

Obviously the main pride in Tom Jones's achievements was felt in Britain, because the old "local-boy-makes-good" yarn was getting so many extra twists. But there were press cuttings galore to prove the amazement Americans felt at the way he'd taken over their show business scene.

As Sue Amon, a television editor, wrote, of her first meeting with Tom Jones: "When he came in, no-one fainted. But the noise level of conversation dropped decidedly when Tom, Wales' sexy singer, entered the room. He had hardly gotten seated and been handed a drink when the questions started coming.

"What had his fans done that really shocked him? He smiled and answered: 'I was in London, on what you would call a freeway and I stopped at a gas station. I went into the restroom and six girls came in right after me.'

"Well, was it true that he and his wife Melinda were getting a divorce? Again the smile and the quick laugh: 'When I left home this morning, everything was all right!'

"So what about all the protestors and demonstrators and young people who wanted peace? Did he identify with them and support their cause? Again, his answer was less than popular maybe but certainly honest. 'I don't believe in all that. I think you should fight for your country. Adults are listening to kids too much. They have to realize that they, the adults, are right sometimes. You have to fight for peace.'

"Now I was a fan of Tom Jones long before seeing him and now that I've seen him, he'll have a place in my scrap-book for ever. I was pleasantly surprised at the way he handled himself with the Press. I had prepared myself for an arrogant, aloof Tom Jones, but what I saw was an honest, relaxed, confident man. The mood of the Press was a little bit vicious. They seemed to be digging for scandal or at least something controversial. It seemed to me that they had all gotten together beforehand and decided to find something that would destroy the hearts of millions of women all over the world.

"One girl writer got almost carried away when she asked Tom if it was true that he had ripped the seam out of his pants during one of his television shows. Tom never flinched. He just said: 'Yes, the pants were tight and I sweat a lot. The seam ripped out okay. Thankfully it was the last number of the show, so I just backed off stage.'

"Afterwards, Tom signed autographs. I was about

second or third in line, not that I was anxious. I handed him the picture, he signed it and handed it back. He smiled. It was the smile that did it. When he smiled at ME, all the poise and sophistication that I'd maintained left me. I didn't faint. I just backed up and ran right into a chair. But that's par for the course."

Look magazine, via assistant editor Betty Baer, described a Tom Jones concert in Wallingford, Connecticut thus: "Crouching inside a crust of cops, Tom hurries down the aisle and bursts onto stage. Local ladies in bra dresses pound on plugs of double Dentyne and clutch at their mouths to hold back the thrill. The billowing tent sounds like a henhouse on a summer night.

". . . For 'Danny Boy,' he is perspiring real good. The women crush forward to hand up their hankies. Tom mops up, then with crowd-thrilling benevolence, tosses back his precious sweat.

"...As Tom skips into view... [a] chain of guards... [t]ime after time ... grab up the women and fling them back like undersized fish. Tom's agent moves among the guards, demanding that no one be hurt. You can't hear Tom sing."

These were typical of scenes that followed Tom everywhere. The British had been reasonably reserved; the Americans had no inhibitions at all.

Tom provided great material at his press conferences: "In my hometown, I think the kids are still growing up in the same way, drinking beer in the same pubs, talking the same language. I can't see it changing. Today, everybody is scared. Scared to death of growing up, scared to death of kids, listening to kids like they have something to say. When I was a teenager, if I tried to tell my old man what to do, he'd tell me to shut up or I'd feel the backside of his hand. He'd say: 'When you're man enough to take me, then come around.'

"I'd wear big shoulder pads, a greatcoat and stick out my chest to try and look as old as I could. I'd take my girl friend to a dance and look every boy straight in the eye and say, 'If you touch her, I'll break your bones'. Then I'd take a cigarette out and light it up like a man. I don't see that happening today.

"Nobody wants to fight, not for his woman, not for his country. They all want the easy way. That's what is wrong with drugs. It takes a man to drink liquor. See, you can get high smoking pot and never get sick. But it takes a man to hold his liquor, or be able to pay the penalty."

Tom really had it made with the press of the United States. They took instantly to a character who could live with his stardom yet remain just the same underneath as when he was a nonentity. And Americans with specialist interests in different aspects of show business liked him because he was setting new standards in entertainment.

"This was the time," wrote Cecil Smith, of the *Los Angeles Times*, "when the worst television we saw came out of England. I'm not referring to the material or the performance, but the sheer physical look of it, the shabby sets, the inept lighting, the makeshift costuming, the bulkiest chorus girls on earth.

"That's all changed and some of the handsomest

shows on the air are made in London—and notable
among them is "This Is Tom Jones."

"This man Jones is built like an oak with thick-
muscled arms from the coal mines of his boyhood in
Wales. With his black shirt, his long thin cigar clinched
between white teeth, the black curls twisting over his
forehead, he was something that caused people on the
street to turn and stare, which they don't often do in
Los Angeles.

"Mostly it was the walk that caught them. Tom walks
with the prideful strut of a matador or a young lion,
master of all he surveys. In an era when performers
look like public accountants or skid-row derelicts, Tom
Jones looks, walks and acts like a star. He found America a fantastic place. But the impact of America on Tom
Jones was no more fantastic than the impact of Tom
Jones on America. He was swarmed over by jewelled
matrons who tossed their room keys on the stage to him
when he played Las Vegas."

So what happened to those hotel-room keys? Writer
Fergus Cashin put the question straight to Tom. He'd
pondered the point thus: What about all this wild adulation from the matriarchal blue-rinsed society of the
United States? What about those slick chicks who
tossed their room keys on stage and socked it to him,
pelvic thrust for pelvic thrust, during his act? Nobody
was going to tell Fergus that a full-blooded male from
Pontypridd was going to ignore that kind of invitation!

And Tom said, "I'm there to unbutton their emotions.
That's what they want. But I tell you, it's all rather
red-faced when the poor husband has to come backstage

to retrieve the key. It's a sexy act, but it is not an act of sex.

"I'm just a singer who is trying to get across to the audience that I am alive and that I am a man. It's as distant as the film actor thing, really. What you're trying to ask is why don't I run off with some beauty. Why the hell should I? Why don't you? I had a nowhere conversation with Eddie Fisher about this subject when I was in Hollywood. He says: 'Tom, I envy you. You are so happy. What's the secret? Where have I gone wrong?' Well, just listening to that gave me a pain. You won't find happiness in marriage through marriages. If you can't make it work, forget it."

This was one of Tom's constant themes. Marriage is giving and taking and trying hard to do things the right way. He had a rather forthright view of the people he met in Hollywood because it seemed to him that they were almost deliberately naive and immature. He said: "When I go home to my wife, she's always going on about curtains or bloody wallpaper and I maybe couldn't care less. It would be easy to say shut up, do what you like but leave me alone. I've said that, but I also realise that this is her life and she makes the life I live. She doesn't dig parts of the show-biz scene but she goes along with it because it's me. I think that is love and I'm lucky. She's tolerant, more so than me. I wouldn't like it much if it was the other way round and she was a singer who was out all the time."

In London the *Daily Mirror* gave Tom a final accolade. Selecting various heroes for 1969, the paper picked Tom Jones as the "Rage of the Year." That he most certainly was a rage, they said, "was echoed by millions of dollies across the world. To them, the Jones voice, huge and husky, vibrates with sex like the frame itself. Tom spells out that word in an instant way. His eyes blaze with it, the grin is gauged to gore out the female heart and the gyrations only serve to force the message relentlessly home.

"In the year when the Welsh miner's son conquered the world of entertainment and won the number one sex symbol stakes, it's left for his wife Linda to say: 'I feel alive when he comes in, whatever time of the day or night it is.' Did you feel the earthquake of a sigh?"

12   1970—Worldwide

By 1970 Tom Jones was a world figure in the strictest interpretation of that tag. It really was a worldwide thing, not just a matter of the United States and Britain. True, there were nonbelievers: "So Tom is okay in America, which is why he spends so much time there. But the novelty will wear off. American womanhood is up there on a pedestal—everything hinges round her likes and dislikes. But it'll wear off."

But the world is bigger than Britain and the United States. Tom was a star in countless countries. In fact, *Billboard* magazine, a long-established and authoritative directory of show business happenings, investigated just how big Tom was in countries not noted for big sales of English-language records.

What emerged was a stack of additional information about a worldwide superstar. The evidence established an important point. Even singing in a "foreign" language, Tom had the sort of magic to make fans of all ages sit up and take notice. In many countries there was only the odd handout photograph to get across his visual impact; Tom just hadn't the time to cart his twitching torso to every country in which his records sold.

In Israel, for instance, Tom started his hit career in the usual way, with "It's Not Unusual." By mid-1970, however, he had hit the top of the charts seven times, and his "Delilah" was voted the most popular foreign song of 1968. Said Gad Barkuz, manager of the company distributing Tom's records: "His popularity in Israel increases all the time. We now release every record he makes as soon as possible, knowing that it will sell well. And we are always after him to make live appearances here."

Tom had sold 10,000 albums by 1970 in Israel, a small number compared with the Gold Discs he'd collected for sales of albums in the United States, but very big sales all the same in that particular market.

In Norway, another country where Tom had not appeared in live shows, though his television series was popular, a representative of his record distributing company said: "He hits every category of record buyer in all age groups and this is one reason for his remarkable success. He just sells and sells."

By 1970 Tom had had three singles in the Norwegian charts, but his main strength was in albums. *Tom Jones Live in Las Vegas* went to the top of the charts. A Silver Disc in Norway was equivalent to a Gold Disc in the United States, and Tom had two silver platters to add to his collection.

In Spain, Tom really broke the record books wide open. Never in the history of the Spanish record industry had an artist beaten his summer, 1968, feat: he had fifteen consecutive weeks at the top of the chart with "Delilah." "Delilah" sold 150,000 copies in Spain, and even local pop heroes rarely reached that total. Before "Delilah," Tom had been at number one for three weeks with "I'm Coming Home," and he had had eleven weeks in the top five with "Help Yourself." As in other parts of the world, 1968 was a winner, one of Tom's biggest and he was voted best "foreign singer" in almost every Spanish poll.

Spanish fans were luckier than most on the Continent. During 1967 Tom appeared in a series of triumphant sellout appearances in Madrid, Barcelona, and Palma de Mallorca. In fact, in 1967 and thereafter there was no question but that Tom was the most popular British singer in Spain.

In Sweden, too, Tom was one of the biggest money-spinners on disc. By the spring of 1970 he had sold a total of 400,000 units there: 240,000 albums, 150,000 singles, and 10,000 cartridges and cassettes.

Moreover, journalist Kjel E. Genberg said: "Because of special peculiarities in the Swedish charts, Tom Jones has had only two singles listed on the Tio I Top, which is a foreign-songs chart compiled from popularity polls. They were 'Green, Green Grass of Home' and 'Love Me Tonight'. But on Kvallstoppen, the chart based on sales, he has scored with a number of releases, including the best-selling album *This Is Tom Jones*. Undoubtedly sales have been stimulated by the Swedish Broadcasting Corporation's showing of thirteen of his television shows."

Tom's only personal appearance in Sweden was in April, 1967, when, with the Squires, he played a concert at the Stockholm Concert Hall. To be honest, the concert was not a success. But his popularity increased fast as the hit records went on—one testimonial to his success was reflected in the large number of Swedish "cover versions" of his songs; several Swedish stars got hits through adapting Tom's material.

Almost every Tom Jones record made the Top Twenty in Switzerland. The list started, once again, with "It's Not Unusual," but "Delilah" was easily his biggest selling single. For a time, however, Tom's disc popularity was in doubt in Switzerland, mainly because he made no personal appearances there (the problem in Switzerland was finding a hall big enough to pack in all the fans who wanted to see Tom). But his popularity boomed again after the slackening of interest.

In Yugoslavia there has never been any doubt that Tom is the most popular foreign singer. His public there, reported journalist Borjan Kostic, ranged from teenagers to grandparents. Two of his albums figured in the Top Ten chart, a unique achievement—"because the album market is minimal and very few albums are issued." Some of Tom's television shows were screened in Yugoslavia. And as Kostic explained: "While people here may not understand the words of his songs, they certainly understand the feelings he conveys. He makes a strong emotional impact which strikes a responsive chord in the Yugoslav people. In general, sophisticated singers make little mark in this country. But Tom Jones, with his powerful voice and simple sincerity, has a very faithful following."

The saga is repetitive—a matter of stunning facts and figures—but its recital is vital to show just how truly *international* was the appeal of the lad from Wales. In Hungary, for example, the fans were turned on because "Delilah" started getting exposure on radio. The song established Tom's following, and several of his shows were later shown on television. So great was public demand, indeed, that the shows were later repeated. The top disc jockey in Hungary, Gyorgy Komjathy, was a regular booster of Tom's records and once devoted an hour of radio time to replay *Live in Las Vegas.*

After the broadcast, thousands of listeners demanded a repeat of the show and the program was rebroadcast nationwide by Radio Kossuth ten days later. This time it went out at the peak hour of 8:00 P.M. Later, the Qualiton company pressed and released, under license, several Tom Jones records.

It was the same story in Holland. Instant acclamation for "It's Not Unusual" led to Tom's being voted easily the most popular foreign singer. "Green, Green Grass" sold more than 100,000 copies and earned him a Gold Disc. "Delilah" was a close runner-up in sales. And even in this small country, his albums all sold around 15,000 copies each. Again, there were no per-

143

sonal appearances to establish his power, just one special forty-five minute television spectacular.

Germany? "Delilah" catapulted Tom to the top of the German charts in 1968 and earned him yet another Gold Disc. His television series was shown in Germany, and he was regarded as a world entertainer, even if he couldn't speak a word of the language.

Another country where Tom became a massive star, largely in absentia, was France. The few personal appearances he did manage to fit in were sellout shows in Paris, and had he been able to undertake a full season at the famed Olympia Theatre, he certainly had enough fans to fill it. After all, his biggest impact came through one-nighter shows at the Olympia in 1966 and 1968, for the Musicorama series. Sales of his records were excellent in France. His singles pulled in totals of anything between 30,000 and 80,000 and albums usually totted up 10,000. "Delilah," that faithless song heroine, sold 300,000 copies, shattering the French record industry.

In Finland, too, Tom hit the top of the charts regularly. "Green, Green Grass" and "Delilah" reached the number one spot in the best sellers, despite some strong competition from local artists covering the same songs.

Reported Kari Helopaltio, a Finnish show business expert: "Jones is one of the very few foreign artists to have made it big in Finland without any personal appearances. Undoubtedly his success could be even more sensational if he could play through a concert tour. But his television shows, put out only once a month, helped sales along and also helped to sell song-books. The *Tom*

Jones Song Album, which sold indifferently at the start, became a sell-out property."

The Finns also voted Tom top male singer; Tom emerged thousands of votes ahead of Elvis Presley. And he has been consistently listed as the most popular singer in bimonthly polls conducted by the teenage magazine *Intro.*

In Denmark, Tom will be a tremendous record seller for just as long as he chooses to put out releases. When "Green, Green Grass" hit it big, Tom appeared in Copenhagen and also made some television appearances. In 1968 he was back again for two standing-room-only concerts at the Tivoli Theatre's 125th anniversary celebrations.

In Belgium all of Tom's records get vast radio exposure on both the Flemish and the Walloon networks— anything up to ten air plays a day. True, in Belgium, Tom was generally rated second to Elvis Presley, but he still racked up a series of 100,000 sellers, among them "Help Yourself," and that is a lot of records for such a small country.

Facts and figures but they all help to prove that Tom was one of the handful to break through the language barrier as well as the generation gap. In Czechoslovakia, in fact, Tom was paid a distinctly unusual tribute. In his book Albert Rosner, professor of the Pop Conservatoire in Prague, described Tom as a model for all pop singers, "a star whose voice measures up to all the classical criteria for singing."

Tom became the most popular singer in Czechoslovakia, as was proved when his British album, *Delilah*, sold 22,000 copies through the Supraphon Record Club series, a new record sale for the organization, beating the Beatles' *Oldies but Goodies*, which drew 15,000 orders. And in Czechoslovakia, again, many Tom Jones hits were covered by local artists.

Tom's European reputation continued to climb while Tom Jones undertook his mammoth, six-month tour of U.S. cities in 1970. No wonder that Gordon Mills once again said: "I said he'd be the biggest and he is. At full international level." And one can understand Gordon's puzzlement when he added: "Yet there are still so many people, even back home in Britain, who really have no idea just how big, how important, Tom is."

The assessment of pop music, since the advent of the sales charts, has all too often been based more on sales statistics than on individual talent. And as everyone knows, there are three kinds of lies: lies, damned lies, and statistics. In Tom's case, however, his vital statistics, in virtually every pop-playing country around the world, are irrefutable.

13 Tom Jones Onstage

Even on Tom Jones's own established stamping grounds, 1970 was to be bigger than anybody could have expected. In March he went off on a tour of his own country. "At last, a Royal gesture . . . in the flesh," reported the *Sunday Mirror*, a reference to the long gaps between Tom's British tours.

That his concerts were a sellout success goes, by now, without saying, and certainly the statement involves no exaggeration. There had been the records, of course, to sustain his fans, but it was Tom in person they wanted and they rolled up to see him in vast halls in Liverpool, Cardiff, London, Birmingham, and Manchester. There were always people telling him he'd chanced his arm by being so long away from his home country, but the sheer warmth of the reception at every whistle convinced Tom that he hadn't lost one iota of his popularity.

Mother sat next to daughter, and they both screamed and yelled and looked stunned. The generation gap was forgotten as they roared their approval of every gnarled note, every hip-locking contortion.

Tom hadn't lost any of the enthusiasm for gyrating like a cement-mixer. Women watched him through binoculars, and they watched him through real tears of adoration and love. Tom just hadn't changed, they noted, and if the mixture was as before, well, it was perfectly all right with the audiences.

After the shows, Tom quickly became involved with Gordon Mills and the others in his party, always looking for ways to improve the act. Indeed, Tom's constant striving for perfection was in direct contrast to so many top pop personalities, who treated their audiences to open-faced contempt and were even more offhand when the curtain was rung down. Tom worried about every musical nuance, and it mattered nothing to him that most of those nuances were lost anyway in the barrage of cheers and screams.

Touring with Tom had something of a ritual character about it: a good meal before going on, preferably a steak or two; every mental and physical ounce of energy in a show or two; a quick postmortem; champagne and conversation into the early morning.

The critics seemed surprised that Tom Jones hysteria was showing no sign of abatement during his long spells away. But the audience reaction was built on a solid formula. Give 'em something to listen to, and never mind if the loud messages outdid the soft passages by a few hundred percent; give 'em something to watch, and that meant a jog-trotting routine; and give the impression that being out on a stage was the one thing above all that he enjoyed doing.

But once again it was to be a short stay in Britain. He soon left for another six-month tour of the United States and once again the box-office records were smashed. One U.S. reporter was amazed to find that Tom clearly still wore the same size in hats. Explaining his view that "no man can have all this adulation and remain the same guy," he went on to say: "This Tom Jones looks like a star and behaves like a star but you get through to him and he's more like the guy next door."

There have seldom, if ever, been scenes in show business to match those witnessed during Tom's performances at the Copacabana. The Copa is a smallish room with a low ceiling, and the stars have to undergo a perilous journey through the body of the room to get from the dressing room to the stage.

The closeness of the audience caused little difficulty for most stars. But when this Jones boy came to town, there was chaos. A long line of waiters, doubling as personal bodyguards, linked arms to prevent American womanhood from busting out all over. One was reminded of a heavyweight boxer being escorted to the ring to do battle for a world title; Tom frequently draped a towel around his neck, over his shoulders.

It was as tricky getting him off the stage afterward —a quick signal from Gordon Mills and then the fast sprint. There could never be a question of Tom's doing an encore; he'd have been torn to pieces. Once there to the stage and once back was enough, and the surprise element must be kept going all the time.

Nothing was spared to create maximum impact: a massive orchestra behind Tom, seats moved so close that he was almost within touching distance of the audience, and an overall feeling that Tom was somehow host to a party—or a religious revival of some kind. A look around the tables each night, any night, revealed the usual Who's Who of show business, plus some old friends, plus a gaggle of rubber-necks who turned out, unconvinced at first, just to see what all the fuss was about.

The scenes of hysteria were shattering. Women jumped on tables and then jumped from table to table. They threw personal possessions—a pair of panties here, a hotel-room key there, even on one occasion a roll of dollar bills. Basically, Tom was a "menace" to every male escort in the place, but they still stayed and listened because he could *sing*.

Each show was worth thousands of dollars to Tom, yet one got the impression that he'd have gone on for nothing just so long as people left him clear to do his act. And he rarely spoke of the hysteria and the crowd chaos. "I always dreamed of being right up there at the top," he'd say. "It was what I always wanted. Now it's happened and I still don't think I can take anything for granted. There's always the next show and the chance that something could go wrong."

What did go a bit wrong was that voice. The multi-million dollar sound sometimes sounded too rough and raw. It was simply the strain: on one occasion Tom did three shows—three hours of tremendous vocal exercise.

In any case, it was back to the specialist and the throat sprays and the tablets. Again, it was the dry air and the dried-up indoor atmosphere that caused the trouble. On one or two occasions thereafter Tom took some of the tougher songs out of his act, but it took a lot more than painful discomfort to make him even think about stopping in full song.

Like Elvis Presley before him, Tom took his own entourage round the United States. Gordon Mills, of course, was there, organizing every item down to the last detail. Tom's press representative, Chris Hutchins, seemed to be everywhere, handing out facts and figures about Tom's progress.

Then, there were a personal assistant, Gordon Jones (like Gordon Mills a one-time bus conductor back home in Wales); a professional boxer from Liverpool, Rocky Seddon, who was technically number-one bodyguard but was also a nice helpful guy who coped with Tom's physical protection; musical director Johnny Spence, one of the most imaginative music men in the business; lead guitarist Big Jim Sullivan, essential to the backing team and one of the most respected figures in the British guitar world; drummer Chris Slade, who laid down the beat hard enough for Tom to hear even through the hubbub of crowd reaction; trumpeter Derek Watkins, who gave the sharp edge to the brassy orchestrations behind Tom; and bassist John Rostill, one of the old Shadows, by no means new to the world of screaming hysteria after his years with Cliff Richard but still open-eyed at the way Tom whipped up the crowds.

Tom sometimes thought about buying a home in the United States, mainly because he was often homesick for his own family. "You do miss all the old things," he said. "It's nice meeting new friends and seeing new places, but you do miss the old things." But Linda also was becoming used to worldwide travel, and she generally managed to visit Tom on tour.

Hearing him talk about the things he missed back home, it was hard to remember that a few minutes earlier he had been bashing relentlessly through one of the sexiest acts in show business. Tom pulverized the competition, but there was no sign of resentment from the longer-established kings of pop. Tom shared a stage with Tony Bennett, for example, both of them having been invited up by Ella Fitzgerald.

While Tom toured the United States, in London the *Daily Mirror* surveyed the vocal talents of top pop singers by asking an operatic coach from the Covent Garden Opera to listen to their albums and then to give his verdict. The coach felt that Tom Jones was really a tenor but that he didn't use his voice particularly well at the top range. He added: "His biggest fault is his inconsistency. He has these disconcerting changes of hoarseness and animal-like crowings. I would hear him out on an audition, but I wouldn't ask him to come back. On the evidence of this record, we wouldn't want him."

If Covent Garden wouldn't have wanted Tom, half of American womanhood wanted him more than anything. Tom was inundated with requests to go to parties, open different functions, chop off his hair and distribute it to orphanages, or just to "sit and talk a while." He shook hands about as often as the President. He smiled most of the time. And never was there a sign that he'd finally cracked and become conceited.

What, finally, is Tom Jones? The analysis of just what made Tom Jones such a sensation went on.

What happened, in the first instance, was clear enough. The beat groups had had it all their own way for too long. A predictable reaction against them set in because it was impossible to present much originality with the invariable lineup of guitars, drums, and lead singer.

In an effort to get away from basic group sounds some groups had become more and more introvert in their approach. They played the music they liked, and to hell with whether the public could grasp what was being produced. Other groups, the less imaginative (musically speaking), purveyed a watery sound, mostly on sing-along songs, which had little to do with sex as it really is. At best, theirs was an antiseptic sex.

The boys looked like girls and at first the girls didn't mind much, but there had to be a reaction. And the reaction was Tom Jones. As Nik Cohn wrote in his fine book, *Pop from the Beginning*: "Tom Jones was true beefcake. He was the son of a miner and he was six foot with huge shoulders and a busted nose. By any standards he was a virile hunk, a throwback, and small mods detested him but their mums adored him."

Of course, before the mothers went for Tom, it had been the youngsters who had gone for him. The mood was right for soul singing and roughness and toughness, and they bought his records. Then when Tom showed himself on television, the women said: "At least he's a pop singer with muscles." Tom in fact, was swept along in the adult reaction against the Mick Jaggers and all they seemed to stand for and as.

153

Another factor was Tom's charisma. There was always that reminder, at a Tom Jones show, of the fervor of the oldtime religion shows. Tom called the tune, and the audience reacted wildly. He had the same crowd command that built the reputations of the top-line preachers of the old school—except that a top preacher could wander freely round the streets of New York, while Tom was generally penned in his dressing room or his hotel suite.

Yet Tom was not merely an amazingly virile and charismatic man; his vocal talent was enormous. In fact, his voice and his appearance complemented each other. Nor did he dissipate his star qualities, his vocal realism and physical magnetism; he didn't worry about writing songs, or playing different instruments or even playing the fool. He got out there and sang, and if he hadn't arrived on the pop scene in 1965, for sure someone would have had to invent him.

Tom would never have lasted as a lead singer in a group. Nobody would have tolerated a professional life that required living in Tom's shadow, and Tom could not have failed to dominate every stage on which he stood. Thus, in the end, he had to make it alone. The solo singer, anyway, has fewer hang-ups. Alone, there's no four- or five-way temperamental split to watch for, as in a group; instead, there is freedom to go any way one wants. So many groups collapsed because the different personalities that made up the groups tugged in different directions.

Finally, Tom made it without gimmicks. After all, there's nothing gimmicky about doing your own thing, being yourself. What really makes the superstar stand out from the ordinary entertainer is that touch of genuine originality. Singers had been sexy on the stage before, but Tom took it to an area of common ground: he appealed to all ages.

When Presley held sway, the adults hummed and haaed and felt there was something grotesque about it all, and they either banished him from their kids' gaze or ignored him and hoped he'd eventually go away. Sinatra got them on the screaming scene, a pencil-slim figure, clutching at the microphone as if for support, and the fans wanted to mother him.

There was never any question of Tom's fans wanting to mother him. He didn't need protection—it was more the fans who needed protecting from his own brand of lethal sex appeal. He got them all going, all the generations of femininity—and he had the males watching, sometimes resentfully, but watching and maybe picking up points.

Someone put it to Tom that when he was working onstage, it looked as if he and his women-packed audience were really making a kind of love to each other. Tom just said that he felt that that was a healthy enough thing, with him just letting loose his own feelings and the others reciprocating. But he got irritated when it was suggested his act was deliberately contrived to stir up mass sexuality. "I do it because I feel like doing it at the time," he said.

Always Tom talked of himself self-mockingly; that anybody could even suggest an ulterior motive for anything he did on stage invariably induced an attitude of wide-eyed wonderment.

Tom was an original, too, in that he took the British

155

brand of show business to America and beat long-established stars there on their own home ground. There had been the Beatles and others, of course, but they appealed to a specific category of the population. Tom was going into the night clubs rather than the dance halls and the campus events, and he went in at top level, the uppermost strata of big-money entertainment. Yet when his fans came to worship, it didn't even seem strange that the star should be a one-time brawler from the valleys of Wales.

Tom Jones, for sure, need never work again. But he will keep driving on, striving for the final perfection. Why? Simply because, like all Welshmen, Tom loves to sing.

Only that love of giving vent to voice sustained him when he earned a few cents a night knocking himself out in some uncomfortable hall, and that love still keeps him going today, as he sings only in the best places and is much too busy ever to find time to count the millions he has amassed.

Sammy Davis, Jr. said: "The guy's a groove. Tom is what is happening today. He's a one-man revolution."

Frank Sinatra said: "He's number one in the world today and I'm his number one fan."

Elvis Presley said: "He's fantastic. There's never been anyone to touch him before."

The Friars Club, the exclusive show business group, said Tom was Entertainer of the Year.

Tom Jones says: "I can only give what I have—and I'm thankful that that is enough for many people."

Discography

Despite the fact that Tom's recording bosses have always said that it is difficult finding just the right material for his special kind of singing style, the Welsh wonder has kept up an amazingly consistent stream of both singles and albums.

He sells big at both levels, probably because the younger fans go for the singles while the older ones buy the albums. A recap of the material available over the years shows that he has recorded a mixture of old standards, investing them with new life despite many previous recordings by other artists, and new songs, tailor-made for him.

In the studios, he is a fast worker who goes in prepared for the session, unlike many of his contemporaries, who prefer to work out ideas and arrangements on the spot.

In the United States his singles since the initial breakthrough have been:

Title	Date	Record
It's Not Unusual/To Wait for Love	Feb., 1965	Parrot 9737
What's New, Pussycat/Once Upon a Time	May, 1965	Parrot 9765
With These Hands/Some Other Guy	Aug., 1965	Parrot 9787
Thunderball/Key to My Heart	Nov., 1965	Parrot 9801
Promise Her Anything/A Little You	Jan., 1966	Parrot 9809
Once There Was a Time/Not Responsible	May, 1966	Parrot 40006
What a Party/City Girl	Aug., 1966	Parrot 40008
Green, Green Grass of Home/If I Had You	Nov., 1966	Parrot 40009
Detroit City/Ten Guitars	Feb., 1967	Parrot 40012
Funny Familiar Forgotten Feelings/I'll Never Let You Go	Apr., 1967	Parrot 40014
Sixteen Tons/Things I Wanna Do	July, 1967	Parrot 40016
I'll Never Fall in Love Again/Once Upon a Time	Aug., 1967	Parrot 40018
I'm Coming Home/The Lonely One	Nov., 1967	Parrot 40024
Delilah/Smile Your Blues Away	Feb., 1968	Parrot 40025
Help Yourself/Day by Day	July, 1968	Parrot 40029

Discography

Title	Date	Record
A Minute of Your Time/ Looking Out My Window	Nov., 1968	Parrot 40035
Love Me Tonight/Hide and Seek	May, 1969	Parrot 40038
Without Love/Man Who Knows Too Much	Dec., 1969	Parrot 40045

Tom Jones's U. S. Albums are:

It's Not Unusual: It Takes a Worried Man; Skye Boat Song; Once Upon a Time; Memphis, Tennessee; Whatcha Gonna Do; I Need Your Loving; It's Not Unusual; Autumn Leaves; If You Need Me; Some Other Guy; Endlessly; It's Just a Matter of Time; Spanish Harlem; When the World Was Beautiful. (Parrot PAS 71004)

A–tom–ic Jones: Dr. Love; Face of a Loser; In a Woman's Eyes; I'll Never Let You Go; Key to My Heart; True Love Comes Only Once in a Lifetime; A Little You; You're So Good for Me; Where Do You Belong; These Things You Don't Forget; Thunderball; Promise Her Anything. (Parrot PAS 71007)

Funny Familiar Forgotten Feelings: Ghost Riders in the Sky; He'll Have to Go; Funny Familiar Forgotten Feelings; Sixteen Tons; Two Brothers; My Mother's Eyes; Ring of Fire; Field of Yellow Daisies; Wish I Could Say No to You; All I Give You Is Heartaches; Mohair Sam; Cool Water; Detroit City. (Parrot PAS 71011)

Tom Jones Live: The Star Theme; Ain't That Good News; Hello, Young Lovers; I Can't Stop Loving You; What's New, Pussycat; Not Responsible; I Believe; My Yiddish Momma; Shake; That Lucky Old Sun; Green, Green Grass of Home; It's Not Unusual; Land of a Thousand Dances. (Parrot PAS 71014)

The Tom Jones Fever Zone: Don't Fight It; You Keep Me Hanging On; Hold On, I'm Coming; I Was Made to Love Her; Keep on Running; Get Ready; Delilah; I Know; I Wake up Crying; Funny How Time Slips By; Danny Boy; It's a Man's Man's Man's World. (Parrot PAS 71019)

Help Yourself: Help Yourself; I Can't Break the News to Myself; The Bed; Isadora; Set Me Free; I Get Carried Away; This House; So Afraid; If I Promise; If You Go Away; My Girl Maria; All I Can Say Is Goodbye; Laura; My Elusive Dreams. (Parrot PAS 71025)

This Is Tom Jones: Fly Me to the Moon; Little Green Apples; Wichita Lineman; The Dock of the Bay; Dance of Love; Hey Jude; Without You; That's All Any Man Can Say; That Wonderful Sound; Only Once; I'm a Fool to Want You; Let It Be Me. (Parrot PAS 71028)

Tom Jones Live in Las Vegas: Turn on Your Love Light; The Bright Lights and You Girl; I Can't Stop Loving You; Hard to Handle; Delilah; Danny Boy; I'll Never Fall in Love Again; Help Yourself; Yesterday; Hey Jude; Love Me Tonight; It's Not Unusual; Twist and Shout. (Parrot PAS 71031)

Discography

Tom: I Can't Turn You Loose; Polk Salad Annie; Proud Mary; Sugar, Sugar; Venus; I Thank You; Without Love; You've Lost That Lovin' Feelin'; If I Ruled the World; The Impossible Dream; Let There Be Love. (Parrot PAS 71037)

Green, Green Grass of Home: Green, Green Grass of Home; A Taste of Honey; Georgia on My Mind; That Old Black Magic; If Ever I Would Leave You; Any Day Now; Someday; You Came a Long Way from St. Louis; My Mother's Eyes; My Prayer; Kansas City; When I Fall in Love. (Parrot PAS 71009)

What's New, Pussycat: What's New, Pussycat; Some Other Guy; I've Got a Heart; Little by Little; One More Chance; Bama Bama Bama Loo; With These Hands; Untrue Unfaithful; To Wait for Love; And I Tell the Sea; The Rose; Endlessly. (Parrot PAS 71006)

Tom Jones received Gold Discs for the following albums: *Tom Jones Live in Las Vegas, This Is Tom Jones, Help Yourself, Tom Jones Live, The Tom Jones Fever Zone,* and *Green, Green Grass of Home.*

He also received Gold Discs for two singles, "Without Love" and "I'll Never Fall in Love Again."